S. R. (Seneca Ray) Stoddard

**The Adirondacks**

Illustrated

S. R. (Seneca Ray) Stoddard

**The Adirondacks**
*Illustrated*

ISBN/EAN: 9783743467040

Manufactured in Europe, USA, Canada, Australia, Japa

Cover: Foto ©Andreas Hilbeck / pixelio.de

Manufactured and distributed by brebook publishing software (www.brebook.com)

S. R. (Seneca Ray) Stoddard

**The Adirondacks**

# THE
# ADIRONDACKS:

## ILLUSTRATED.

BY

S. R. STODDARD,

Author of

"Ticonderoga," "Lake George, Illustrated," etc.

---

ALBANY:
WEED, PARSONS & CO., Printers
1874.

Entered, according to act of Congress, in the year 1874,

By S. R. STODDARD,

In the office of the Librarian of Congress, at Washington.

# CONTENTS.

|  | PAGE. |
|---|---|
| GENERAL INDEX—Summer Resorts, Hotels, etc. | iv |
| Lakes and Ponds | iv |
| Mountains | v |
| Miscellaneous | v |
| Illustrations | vi |
| THANKS | vii |
| ROUTES, Distance Tables, etc. | 155 |
| FARES to Different points | 161 |
| TIME TABLES—R. & S. R. R. | 164 |
| Champlain Steamers | 165 |
| Vermont Central | 166 |
| MAPS—The Great Wilderness | In Cover |
| Railroad Map | 163 |
| Schroon Lake | 190 |
| Ausable Chasm | 44 |
| GUIDES, Names and Post-office Address | 151 |
| CALENDAR.—Modesty | 200 |

CHAPTER I.—IN GENERAL—Outfit—Supplies—Guides—Expenses.
CHAPTER II.—LAKE CHAMPLAIN—Past and Present—Whitchall—Ticonderoga—Plattsburgh.
CHAPTER III.—NARRATIVE—The Start—The Pilot—"Well, by Thunder!"
CHAPTER IV.—AUSABLE CHASM—Keeseville—Wilmington.
CHAPTER V.—WHITEFACE MOUNTAIN—The Ascent—"Little Foot-prints"—Down the Mountain.
CHAPTER VI.—ON THE ROAD—Wilmington Pass—"Gr-roop"—John Brown—North Elba—At the Grave—A Woman of Business.
CHAPTER VII.—LAKE PLACID—Att's Humor—Paul Smith's—The First Snow Storm—Martin's.
CHAPTER VIII.—THE LOWER SARANAC—Round Lake—Bartlett's—A tired Clerk—The Upper Saranac—Encounter with a Fish-ball—Tupper Lake Region—Up the Raquette—Long Lake.
CHAPTER IX.—RAQUETTE LAKE—The Schoolmaster—The Carry—Forked Lake—The Raquette—Marion River.
CHAPTER X.—THE EAGLE'S NEST—Ned Buntline—Blue Mountain Lake—Over the Mountain—Newcomb.
CHAPTER XI.—ON THE TRAMP—John Cheney—Adirondack, the Ruined Village—Avalanche Lake—"Bill Nye"—"Hitch up, Matilda."
CHAPTER XII.—INDIAN PASS—From Lake Henderson to North Elba.
CHAPTER XIII.—PLEASANT VALLEY—Elizabethtown.
CHAPTER XIV.—KEENE FLATS—"The Old Man of the Mountains"—Ausable Ponds—Panther Gorge—Mount Marcy—Good-bye to the Mountains.
CHAPTER XV.—GUIDES—Names, Post-office Address, etc.
CHAPTER XVI.—ROUTES—Excursions—Tables of Distance—Fares, etc.
CHAPTER XVII.—SUMMER RESORTS—Miscellaneous.

# INDEX.

## SUMMER RESORTS.

| | PAGE. | | PAGE. |
|---|---|---|---|
| AUSABLE CHASM—Chasin House, | 44, 169 | MOOERS | 175 |
| CHESTERTOWN | 189 | NORTH ELBA | 74, 170 |
| ELIZABETHTOWN | 132, 173 | NEWCOMB—Half-way House, | 113, 171 |
| GLENS FALLS | 181 | PLATTSBURGH—Fouquet's Hotel, | 26, 167 |
| KEESEVILLE | 52, 168 | POTTERSVILLE HOTEL | 192 |
| KEENE FLATS—Dibble's | 135, 174 | RAQUETTE FALLS | 94 |
| Crawford's | 136, 176 | ROOT'S HOTEL | 192 |
| LONG LAKE | 100, 172 | ST. REGIS LAKE | 80, 169 |
| LAKE PLACID—Nash's | 75, 170 | LOWER SARANAC | 83, 169 |
| Brewster's | 75, 170 | UPPER SARANAC | 86, 169 |
| LAKE GEORGE—Fort William Henry Hotel | 183 | SARATOGA—Congress Hall | 177 |
| | | Remedial Institute | 179 |
| Central Hotel | 14, 184 | SCHROON LAKE—Leland House, | 193 |
| Crosbyside | 185 | Wickham House | 194 |
| Mohican House | 186 | Ondawa House | 195 |
| Bolton House | 187 | Taylor House | 195 |
| Fourteen Mile Island | 188 | TUPPER'S LAKE | 91, 171 |
| LUZERNE | 180 | TICONDEROGA HOTEL | 15 |
| MUD POND | 195 | WHITEFACE MOUNTAIN | 55, 171 |

## LAKES AND PONDS.

| | | | |
|---|---|---|---|
| Avalanche Lake (el. 2,846) | 122 | Mud Pond | 195 |
| Ausable Ponds | 140, 142 | Placid (el. 1,947) | 75, 170 |
| Blue Mountain Lake | 112 | Preston Ponds | 120 |
| Champlain (el. 95) | 91 | Pleasant (el. 1,578). | |
| Chazy Lake | 33 | Paradox Pond | 76 |
| Chateaugay Lake | 33 | Raquette Lake | 105 |
| Cranberry Lake | 93 | Round Lake | 86 |
| Colden (el. 2,747) | 122 | Upper Saranac | 88, 169 |
| Calamity Pond | 121 | Lower Saranac | 84, 169 |
| Eldon | 108 | St. Regis Lake | 79, 169 |
| Forked Lake | 104 | Sanford | 117 |
| George | 183 | Summit Water (el. 4,293) | 146 |
| Henderson | 127 | South Pond | 112 |
| Long Lake (el. 1,584) | 96, 172 | Schroon Lake | 191 |
| Mirror Lake | 75 | Tupper's Lake (el. 1,504) | 92 |
| Mud Lake (el. 1,737) | 92 | Utowanna Lake | 109 |

# INDEX.

## MOUNTAINS.

| | PAGE. | | PAGE. |
|---|---|---|---|
| Blue Mountain (el. 3,595) | 112 | Mount Joseph (el. 1,200) | 113 |
| Bald Peak (Moriah) (el. 2,083) | 175 | Marcy (el. 5,333) | 2, 144 |
| Bartlett Mountain | 143 | Mansfield, Vt. (el. 4,350) | 21 |
| Camel's Hump, Vt. (el. 4,080) | 21 | Owl's Head (el. 2,789) | 97 |
| Colvin | 139, 140 | Resagonia Mountain | 139 |
| Colden (el. 4,707) | 127 | Seward (el. 4,348) | 97 |
| Cobble Hill | 132 | Santanona Mountain (el. 4,607) | 127 |
| Gray Peak (el. 4,947) | 146 | Whiteface (el. 4,918) | 56, 63 |
| Gothic Mountains | 142 | Rustic Lodge (Whiteface) (el. 4,080) | 57 |
| Giant, The | 139 | Wallface Mountain (el. 3,856) | 129 |
| Haystack | 143 | (Height of Precipice, 1,319.) | |
| Hurricane | 132 | Washington, N. H. (el. 6,285). | |
| Indian Head | 140 | | |

## MISCELLANEOUS.

| | PAGE. | | PAGE. |
|---|---|---|---|
| Ausable Chasm | 45 | Keene Flats | 134, 168 |
| List of Views | 200 | Long Lake Village | 97 |
| Adirondack Iron Works (el. 1,769) | 118 | Lumbermen | 111 |
| Adirondack Springs | 20, 175 | Lake George | 183 |
| Arnold Ore Bed | 33 | Marion River | 108 |
| Avalanche Pass | 124 | Mud Pond | 150 |
| Burlington | 21 | Murray's Island | 106 |
| Bloomingdale | 76 | Marcy Trail | 142, 150 |
| Battle of Plattsburgh | 30, 32 | Mould & Son, W | 54, 199 |
| Beech's Island | 107 | Modesty | 200 |
| Buntline, Ned | 110 | North Elba | 71 |
| Buttermilk Falls | 104 | Newcomb | 113, 171 |
| Bill Nye, his Story | 123 | Outfit | 3 |
| Carillon | 18 | Ointments | 6 |
| Crown Point | 19 | Opalescent Gorge | 120 |
| Clinton Prison | 32 | "Old Mountain Phelps" | 137 |
| Champlain Transportation Co. | 11, 165 | Ouluska Pass (el. 3,050) | 146 |
| Cold River | 96 | Plattsburgh | 24, 167 |
| Chateaugay Falls | 33 | Port Kent | 23 |
| John Cheney | 116 | Port Henry | 19 |
| Camp Phelps | 147 | Pleasant Valley | 131, 173 |
| Deadwater | 133 | Panther Gorge | 143 |
| Del. & Hudson Canal Co. | 12, 164 | Phelp's Falls | 135 |
| Elizabethtown | 131 | Pilot, The | 38 |
| Euba Dam | 132 | Photographs, Lists, etc. | 51, 53, 178, 200 |
| Guides | 7, 151 | E. & H. T. Anthony & Co. | 197 |
| Hudson River (Head) | 143 | R. Walzl | 198 |
| Harper & Tufts | 53, 168 | Photo-Engraving Co | 176 |
| Indian Pass (el. 2,901) | 128 | Rouse's Point | 24 |
| Indian Carry | 93 | Roaring Brook | 139 |
| John Brown | 67 | Roaring Brook Falls | 139 |
| John Brown's Grave | 71 | Russle Falls | 139 |
| John's Brook | 135 | Rainbow Falls | 141 |
| Keeseville | 51 | Raquette River | 95 |

## vi                 INDEX.

### MISCELLANEOUS — (Continued).

|  | PAGE. |
|---|---|
| Rock Dunder | 21 |
| Routes | 155 |
| Steamboats | 11, 165 |
| Supplies | 7 |
| Split Rock | 20 |
| Split Rock Falls | 132 |
| Spectacle Ponds | 93 |
| Stony Creek | 94 |
| Sweeny Carry | 91 |
| Sheridan, Gen. Phil | 40 |
| Sabattis, Mitchell | 99 |
| The Schoolmaster | 101 |
| Tupper Lake Region | 91 |
| Ticonderoga | 15 |
| Tahawus (P. O.) | 114 |
| Vermont Central R. R. | 12, 166 |
| Whitehall | 12 |
| Westport | 20 |
| Wilmington (el. 1,021) | 55, 171 |
| Wilmington Pass | 64 |
| Wilmington Flume | 64 |

### ILLUSTRATIONS.

| | |
|---|---|
| Ausable Pond | Frontispiece |
| Ticonderoga | 15 |
| Fouquet's Hotel | 26 |
| Floral Offering, A | 29 |
| Battle of Plattsburgh | 30 |
| The Night Express | 35 |
| Professor, Ye | 37 |
| "Lo" | 41 |
| "Well, by Thunder" | 44 |
| Ausable Chasm | Facing 45 |
| Birmingham Falls | 48 |
| "Moses" | 49 |
| Cathedral Rocks | 50 |
| Ausable House | 52 |
| Whiteface Mountain, Summit | 56, 58 |
| "Gr-roop" | 65 |
| John Brown | 67 |
| Wilmington Pass, from the south | 64 |
| John Brown's Grave | 71 |
| Paul Smith's | 78 |
| Martin's | 83 |
| Saranac Lake | 84 |
| Hartlett's | 86 |
| Mother Johnson's | 94 |
| Mother Johnson | 95 |
| Up the Raquette | 95 |
| Mitchell Sabattis | 99 |
| The Schoolmaster | 102 |
| The Carry | 102 |
| Alva Dunning's | 107 |
| "Ned Buntline" | 111 |
| Blue Mountain Lake | 112 |
| John Cheney | 117 |
| Adirondack | 118 |
| Lake Sanford, Wallface in Distance | 117 |
| Wm. B. Nye | 123 |
| "Hitch up, Matilda" | 126 |
| Indian Pass, from Henderson Lake | 127 |
| Indian Pass | Facing 128 |
| South from Blin's | 130 |
| "Where did we put them?" | 133 |
| "Old Mountain Phelps" | 137 |
| Ausable Pass | 140 |
| Gothic Mountains | 142 |
| "Stories" (Camp Phelps) | 147 |
| Tail-piece—The Great Peaks | 150 |
| Exeunt Guides | 154 |

## THANKS.

TO Dr. G. W. Bixby of Plattsburg, for prized suggestions and assistance; to Hon. A. W. Holden of Glens Falls; to Editor Lansing of the Essex Co. *Republican;* to O. S. Phelps of Keene Flats, for a host of literary matter that none were better able than he to give; to Theo. White for those inimitable pan-cakes; to William B. Nye of North Elba; to Charles W. Blanchard of Long Lake, for valuable tables and other matter; to H. G. Baldwin of Whiteface Mountain; to H. M. Mould of Keeseville; to H. H. Bromley of the Chasm House; to L. M. Fouquet of Plattsburgh, for an immense amount of documentary and personal information concerning the great wilderness, of which he has been, for years, an enthusiastic student; to the Delaware & Hudson Canal Co., for interesting material and assistance aside from their duties as carriers; to Weed, Parsons & Co. of Albany, for favors extended, generous uprightness in dealing, and more than satisfaction given in the unvarying excellence of their productions, and to a host of other friends whose names and kindnesses will recur when too late for this public testimonial of appreciation, thanks are given in all sincerity by

THE AUTHOR.

GLENS FALLS, June, 1874.

It was expected that a map sketch of the Adirondack, as prepared by Verplanck Colvin, Superintendent of the Adirondack Survey, could have been procured for this work. The reason of its non-appearance is explained by the accompanying note:

ALBANY, *July* 1, 1874.

S. R. STODDARD, Esq.,

DEAR SIR — I regret that it is impossible to procure a proof of the map sketch promised you to copy. It will accompany my forthcoming report to the legislature on the progress of the Survey, but is not, as yet, completely engraved.

Yours, etc.,

VERPLAŃCK COLVIN.

# THE ADIRONDACKS.

## CHAPTER I.

Fizz-z-z-z ——— pop?

ON wings of thought swifter than the lightning's flash cleaving through space, we sweep away across the drowsy earth, over smoke-polluted cities, sun-scorched meadows, burning plain and highways with their flaunting skirts of sand, nor rest until the fragrant odor of wild flowers and the dewy breath of forest trees come like incense wafted to us from below.

Come with me up into a high mountain! I cannot show you "all the kingdoms of the world," but, "the glory of them." Over a rippling ocean of forests first, their long swelling waves, now rising, now sinking down into deep hollows, here in grand mountains, crested as with caps of foam, there tormented by counter currents into wildly dashing shapes, like ocean billows, frozen by Divine command, their summit-glittering granite, their deep green troughs, gleaming with threads of silver and bits of fallen sky.

Now, the trees of the valley glide away behind us; the dark spruce and pine; and the sturdy balsam climbing the mountain-side — tall and graceful at first, but growing smaller as they rise; now gnarled and twisted and scarce above the surface, sending their branches out close along the ground, their white tops bleached and ghastly, like dead roots of upturned trees, the hardy lichens still higher, then comes naked rock, and we stand on the wind-swept summit of the monarch of the Adirondacks' "Tahawas," the cloud-splitter of the Indian.

Around their chief cluster the other great peaks — East, West, North, South, limitless, numberless, a confused mass of peaks and ridges, gathering, crowding close up to the base of the one on which we stand, and receding in waves of deep, then tender green, all down through the scale of color to its blue and purple edge; pen cannot convey an idea of its sublimity, the pencil fails to even suggest the blended strength and delicacy of the scene. The rude laugh is hushed, the boisterous shout dies out on reverential lips, the body shrinks down, feeling its own littleness, the soul expands, and rising above the earth, claims kinship with its Creator, questioning not his existence.

Standing on this, the highest point in the State of New York, 5,333 feet above tide, we will glance at the country around; the term, at first given to this cluster of mountains, occupying, as they do, less than one-quarter of the region, has come by usage to mean the entire wilderness, covering an area of over 2,500 square miles of almost unbroken forest. The grand mountain region is in the center on the East, dropping off suddenly into Lake Champlain; around it, and sweeping away to the West is a vast, comparatively level plateau, nearly 2,000 feet above tide, with here and there a mountain peak overlooking the plain below, the two regions differing in every respect, save in the dense forests that cover both; if given to muscular exercise, climbing and viewing nature from high places, choose the eastern portion; if constitutionally tired, or inclined to dream away the quiet hours; then go to the magnificent West, where will be found a system of rivers, lakes and streams, so closely connected, that almost every mile of that vast tract may be visited without leaving the boat, save to carry a short distance from one water system into another, around some fall, or to camp for the night, and camping is not necessary if you prefer hotel life, for there are but few wilderness routes that do not have their halting places less than a day's journey apart.

## IN GENERAL; OUTFIT.

The various subdivisions are, first, the mountains on the east. The Raquette and Long Lake region toward the southwest, and still further away the John Brown tract. To the north-west is the Saranac; west of this the Tupper's Lake, Oswegatchie and Grass River regions; north of the Saranac, the St. Regis, and still further north the Chateaugay woods.

It is difficult to say just which part combines the most attractions. The artist finds grandeur among the mountains and quiet loveliness in the Raquette region. The Brown tract is tame, but good fishing; the north-west rather gloomy, but probably the best hunting-ground in the wilderness. The Saranac and St. Regis is the most fashionable and easiest reached. Scattered all over this wild tract are places of entertainment, ranging all the way from the elegantly furnished hotels on the border to the rude log-house of the interior, but all "hotels," and willing to take strangers in at from $2.50 per day to $7.00 per week. "Martin's" is the largest; "Paul Smith's" the most fashionable. Keene Flats has the greatest number of artists — and quiet people.

The avenues of approach radiate to all points of the compass, the favorite being — for the mountain region, by way of Schroon Lake and Root's, or on Champlain steamers to Westport; thence to Elizabethtown and Keene Flats. To the lake region via Lake Champlain steamers, north and south, to Port Kent or Plattsburgh; thence to either the St. Regis or Saranac Lakes, where boats are taken for the interior. Nearly all the hotels advertise to furnish guides, boats and necessaries for camping.

OUTFIT. — Claw hammer coat, fancy vest, bell-muzzle trowsers, stove-pipe hat, lavender kids, tender neckties, perfumery, eye-glasses, cane, is "a stunnin' make-up, by jove," for some; others, however, prefer a coat to button close up in the neck, with "lots" of pockets; with pants and vest of some sort of woolen goods; pair of woolen shirts, soft felt hat, two pairs of woolen socks, pair of heavy kip boots, with broad soles and heels, one or two sizes larger than is ordinarily worn, common carpet slippers, with cloth tops that may be tied outside the pants, for camp and night use, rubber overcoat or blanket, and pair of rubber leggings or overalls.

As to a lady's "outfit," I would not presume to dictate; I have learned better; but the following is suggested as the proper thing for the woods and mountains: Flannel underclothing, short walking dress, Turkish trowsers, buttoned at the ankle, soft felt hat, such as is worn by gentlemen, roomy balmoral boots, camp slippers, rubbers, water-proof, cotton or kid gloves, with armlets to button at the elbow.

The nights are often chilly, and, for sleeping in camp, a pair of heavy woolen blankets are recommended; some make them into a bag about six feet long and three broad, with a cord run in at the top so that it may be shured up around the owner's neck; once in this he can bid defiance to predatory bugs, and need not fear that his bed-fellows will kick the bed-clothes off along in the cold hours of the morning. On the other hand it may not tend toward a devotional feeling when the musical mosquito directs his attention toward your unprotected nose. You can let him take his fill, if you choose, after which he will go off and not molest you again until he finds some of his hungry relations, or you may knock your proboscis against a convenient tree, and hurl the vandal from his giddy height. In the latter case, however, it requires considerable skill to properly gauge the blow. At such trying moments either the hands must have outlet or the feelings will. A pair of sleeves, closed at the end, helps the matter some, but in the construction of the garment a wide field, or rather bag, is still open for the display of inventive genius. A small bag to be filled with leaves or grass, and used as a pillow, pays for itself in one night's use. All the articles enumerated, with, perhaps, the exception of the envelope, may be packed in a valise or knapsack, or, what will answer equally well, a common grain-bag, with two straps attached about half way up, which, passing over the shoulders and back, under the arms, fasten to the lower corners, the load resting well down on the back; don't forget soap, towels and a drinking cup, either of tin or of leather that will flatten down and be carried easily in the pocket. A compass is a very pleasant companion, and at times very useful; needles and thread, pins, and pocket mirror in which to look occasionally, if you are given to *amour propre*. It would be well also to take bandages, lint, ointment, ammonia (often soothing the irritation when applied to blotches caused by the bite or sting of insects), and some kind of cholera medicine; for burns apply wheat flour; to stop the flow of blood from wounds, bind on equal parts of flour and common salt; beware of bulky luxuries or much extra clothing; they are a nuisance and provoke a rebellious spirit in the breast of the guide, for guides even have some rights that their employers are bound to respect.

SPORTING OUTFIT. Do not rely on what books tell you. If you know nothing about it, place yourself under some one that does and trust to their judgment until you can judge for yourself. The most enticing of fancy flies in the hands of a greenhorn will not yield much sport — except to outsiders — and the grandest achievement in patent double acting firearms will not alone deplete the ranks of the timid deer as rapidly as a common rifle backed by common sense and the necessary ammunition, or a fowling piece if you are not skilled in the use of the former; in either case have none but a breech-loader.

The Adirondack Fire Arms Company, of Plattsburgh, make a very popular rifle, which, taken altogether, is probably the best in use, being a "magazine gun" made to contain from seven to seventeen cartridges which are thrown up into the barrel, without removing the gun from the shoulder, by a rapid motion that at the same time casts out the empty shell; one peculiar advantage is its adjustable gauge whereby cartridges of any length can be used — the want of which in others has been a frequent source of annoyance to hunters.

The Rev. Mr. Murray (whose book has been so mercilessly criticised by those who did not possess the first requisite of the sportsman to whom it appealed, and who were misled thereby expecting to see deer in droves and trout in schools coming up to the parlor windows to be shot and hooked, who in His exuberance of spirit may have inflated the unpoetical truth a little at times), is a thorough sportsman and suggests the following for the guidance of fishermen:

FLIES, Hackles, black, red and brown, 6 each; hooks, 1, 2, 3, Limerick size, also 6 Canada flies, 6 green drake, 6 red ibes,

6 small salmon flies (best of all); In the fall of the year, half a dozen each of English blue jay and gray drake, one light, single-handed fly rod, Landing net; he also suggests for boat-fishing two dozen short-shanked good-sized hooks, hand-tied to strong cream-colored snells; for bait use worms, grubs or cut a piece from a chub and troll or skitter it across the surface of the water. Mr. Murray further says, use braided silk lines and invokes you to beware of such as have a glassy glitter about them.

OTHER FLIES. — The black-fly, "punkey"— fearful form of torment conjured up by a diseased mind, owes a great share of its importance to the imagination of writers who do not want to spoil a good story for lack of strength, and so uncork their vials of descriptive terror and cry "black-fly" all because a poor, little, innocent creature, may occasionally take toll from a passing traveler, in a perfectly legitimate manner, in broad daylight. He can't be so very terrible, and when night comes, he retires in a very christian-like manner and does not molest or make you afraid until daylight appears once more, passing away almost entirely early in July. The *mosquito*, however, is a different enemy to deal with, he comes like a thief in the night and presents his bill at the most inopportune moments imaginable, and he is ably supported by the gnat.

To avoid these pests as far as possible select for a camping place some island or point where the open forest affords the wind free sweep. A tent that can be made tight is the best; smudge the insects out, then cover the entrance with thin muslin. As a further protection, take gloves as suggested in ladies' outfit and Swiss muslin bag to cover the head, gathered around the neck and fastened inside the collar band. Ointments of various kinds are also used; the easiest carried perhaps of any is a piece of mutton tallow previously melted, and mixed with oil of pennyroyal in the proportion of six ounces of tallow to one of the oil, to which a little camphor may be added, if preferred; a mixture of sweet oil and tar is also used, with which the face and hands are anointed — tar doesn't look very attractive and is objected to by some ladies, but it is very efficacious, it keeps the flies at a distance and the young men soon get accustomed to it.

SUPPLIES. — Provisions may be obtained at the hotels; but as some prefer to carry them, the following are suggested as the staples: Boston crackers, Indian meal, oat meal (excellent for griddle cakes), baking powder, or what is perhaps better, self-raising flour, maple sugar, loaf sugar (easy to sort if it gets scattered), tea, coffee (condensed milk is good sometimes), dried fruit, pepper, salt, butter. Pint tin cups, tin plates, spoons, knives and forks, two long handle frying-pans, tin basins, two tin pails, holding from three to six quarts each, to be used for tea, coffee, etc.

Bacon is easily carried, and nice, when it *is nice;* but see that it is not rusty when taken; above all, have plenty of salt pork, unpoetical but palatable, taking the place of butter and all of the seasonings. From experience, I have learned that the amount of salt pork a delicate young creature — who before revolted, perhaps, at mention of it — gets away with in the woods, is simply enormous; and then it's "awfully jolly, you know," to broil a piece on a sharp stick, letting the gravy drip on crisp-toasted bread, and eat the two together, no matter if it does drop in the ashes once in a while, it is healthy, and that is the great *desideratum.*

GUIDES usually furnish boat with all necessaries for camping, do all the work, cooking, etc., and carry the boat over all portages (excepting where they are snaked across by horse-power, for which the employer pays) at from $2.50 to $3 per day.

An ordinary boat will carry two beside the guide, and many go in couples, thus lessening expenses in guide-hire one-half; but, for the sake of independence, each person should have his own. There are two classes, known as the "hotel" and "independent guides." The latter, as a rule, give the best satisfaction, not because there are not just as good men among the "hotel" guides as the others, but they are engaged for the season by hotel proprietors, who relet them to parties; and while two or three, out of a half-dozen, may be first-class, the rest are often young and inexperienced — cheap hands sent along to learn the business. I have tried both, and it is not difficult, all other things being equal, to decide who will try to please you most; the one who receives his pay and is responsible to another man for his actions, or the one who looks to you for future employment. Many engage them a year in advance, and would as soon think of going without a gun as their favorite guide.

EXPENSES. — The cost of a trip of course cannot be fairly estimated, varying with the habits and requirements of those taking it. The one described in the narrative portion of this work includes, in its round, over 200 miles by rail, steamboat and stage, 100 by boat, and something more than 100 on foot, the main line, taking in Ausable chasm, Whiteface mountain, Wilmington Notch, John Brown's grave at North Elba, Lake Placid, Paul Smith's and back to Martin's by private conveyance, thence by boat through the Saranac's over to the Raquette, up that and through Long Lake, thence around through Forked, Raquette and Blue Mountain lakes; by mountain carry to Kellogg's once more, then east to Newcomb, north to the deserted village, through Indian Pass to North Elba again, then east to Keene, south through the "Flats" to the Ausable Ponds, thence out to Root's and home by way of Schroon Lake and Lake George, occupying a little over three weeks in the round, and costing — railroad fares, etc., — all told, about $65 each, for the "Professor" and myself; and remember this was for *sight seeing*, during which time we slept in a shanty but one night, then only from choice, and all the time with hotel fare and prices.

From four to five dollars per week is amply sufficient to cover the expenses of any one reasonable being while in the woods, including guide-hire and the little luxuries that have to be taken in, or procured at the hotels. Fares to different points will be found under their appropriate heading, by which an estimate can be made of the total expense of the trip.

## CHAPTER II.

### LAKE CHAMPLAIN.

HE first white sporting man that ever visited the Adirondacks was Samuel de Champlain, a Frenchman, who, in 1609, joined a company of native tourists on a gunning expedition to the southern borders of the future State park, where he fell in with a party of Iroquois and succeeded in bagging a satisfactory number. Samuel, besides being an enthusiastic sportsman, was of a vivacious, happy disposition, as witness his felicitous description of the manner in which he, at the first shot, brought down three out of four Aborigines, who broke cover, then pursued and killed some others; he should, however, receive no credit as a marksman, for he used a beastly arm called an "arquebus," a remote progenitor of the terrible blunderbuss — a shot-gun, which same, I think, all will agree is beneath the dignity of a true sportsman to point toward such game. After this adventure, which happened the same year that Hendrick Hudson sailed up the river that now bears his name, and eleven years before the original pilgrims landed on Plymouth rock, he returned home and wrote an interesting account of the affair, calling the sheet of water explored after himself — Lake Champlain. Just two centuries after his passage in a canoe, the first steamboat was launched on the lake. When he came, the Indians called it *Cani adere quarante*, spelled in various ways, and said by learned authorities who copy it from some one else, to mean "the lake that is the gate of the country." By the early French who did not choose to recognize Champlain's right to the name, it was known as *Mere les Iroquois*, or "Iracosia." A book published in 1659 speaks of it as "the lake of Iroquois, which, together with a river of the same

name, running into the river of Canada, is sixty or seventy leagues in length. In the lake are four fair islands, which are low and full of goodly woods and meadows, having store of game for hunting. Stagges, Fallow Dear, Elks, Roe Bucks, Beavers, and other sorts of beasts." In shape it is very like a long, slim radish, with Whitehall at the little end; then comes the long root and outbranching river fibers. At Burlington, quite a respectable radish, then blotches of rock and island, and, beyond that, the leaves spreading out on either side and toward the North.

On the east is Vermont, sweeping away from the lake in a broad, cultivated plain, then gradually ascending to the ridges of the Green mountains; along the southern and central portion of the lake, the rocky western shores step down to the water's edge and backward, rising up peak on peak the highest, misty with distance or hidden by the clouds that gather around; then wild, broken and grand, the Adirondack mountains. Here and there are little bits of cultivated land and breaks in the mountain-gateways to the wilderness, then as you near Burlington, they fall away back into the interior, and a level, well-cultivated country presents itself.

It is 130 miles from the head of navigation to Rouse's Point; measuring down into Missisquoy bay, on the east side, the extreme length is about 140 miles. It is ninety-one feet above tide, according to late measurements, and the United States Coast Survey shows that a ship drawing 333 feet would barely float in the deepest places, which are near Burlington. Just north of this is the broadest part, the lake being eleven miles across. It contains a number of islands, the principal ones near the north end, where there is plenty of room for them, and contemplating this just distribution of land, in places where it would be least in the way, we are led to think that "whatever is, is right," for had Grand Isle been dropped down in some narrow portion of the lake — Whitehall, for instance, it would have been pretty hard on the inhabitants of that unhappy place, although, perhaps, aside from its lumber, the world would not have felt the loss very keenly.

As of old, "the gate of the country," Lake Champlain, is now a great highway of commerce and pleasure travel, the chief industry being the iron found in large quantities, and of a superior quality, in the mountains on the west shore, and the lumber from the forests of Canada that pass through toward the south. If, as is proposed, the Champlain canal, between Troy and Whitehall, be enlarged, so that vessels of 1,000 tons burden can pass through, it will bring almost the entire freight of the great lakes this way, reducing the time from Oswego to Troy, by canal, about one-quarter, and rendering the transhipment of the cargo to smaller boats unnecessary; the wished-for result, however, is not yet. Men can measure the distance to the planets, track the erratic comet through unknown space and foretell its coming, but the doings of the New York Legislature are past finding out.

THE CHAMPLAIN TRANSPORTATION COMPANY have fully supplied the wants of the traveling public in the magnificent steamers that double the lake daily. This company was organized in 1826, and now run six steamers, viz.: The Vermont, Adirondack, Champlain, A. Williams, Minnehaha, and Ganouskie — the last two on Lake George. Le G. B. Cannon is President; F. P. Noyes, Treasurer; A. L. Inman, General Superintendent, and Elijah Root, Chief Engineer. The first three boats run regular trips the entire length of the lake, day and night; leaving Whitehall and Rouse's Point on the arrival of morning and evening trains. Meals are furnished on board; each boat carries a crew of about 50 persons; consumes 35 tons of coal daily, and will easily make 20 miles an hour. They are of beautiful build, clean and well conducted, with richly furnished state-rooms, and plenty of sitting-room out on the open decks, designed especially for pleasure travel; lacking the tawdry glitter of some steamers, but perfect models of elegance and rich simplicity.

The "VERMONT" was built in 1871, at Shelburne harbor, where all are laid up for the winter; is 262 feet long, 36 foot beam, 9 foot hold, with a capacity of 1,125 tons.

The "ADIRONDACK," built in 1867; length 251 feet; beam, 34; hold, 9; capacity, 1,088 tons.

The "CHAMPLAIN," originally the "Oakes Ames," built in 1868, for the R. R. ferry, between Burlington and Plattsburgh; would carry a half-dozen cars at a trip, and was nearly all hole, with a thin shell of cabin, engine and paddle-wheels around it. In the winter of 1873-74 it was altered over, and is now one of the regular through line; length, 244 feet; beam, 34 feet; hold, 9 feet; capacity, 1,246 tons.

Two great railroad companies join in bringing travel this way; first, the DELAWARE AND HUDSON CANAL COMPANY, a strong and wealthy corporation, who own or lease the Albany & Susquehanna, Rensselaer & Saratoga, and New York & Canada railroads, and branches, and have placed them among the best running, most perfectly appointed roads in the country. Throughout the season of pleasure travel special fast trains are run with drawing-room cars, on all through trains between New York, Albany, Saratoga, Glens Falls and Whitehall, affording a restful change from the boat at Albany, passing through a pleasant country, full of historic interest, and before the pleasurable first sensations of "riding on the rail" has worn away, leaving for the lovely, ever-changing scenery of the narrows — then out into the broad expanse of Lake Champlain.

And right here let me say to you by all means see the "Hudson by daylight" from the deck of some one of the steamers that ply regularly between New York and Albany, where, with Thursty McQuill's book in hand (the which, while undoubtedly the best guide of the route ever published, is at the same time rich in the legendary lore of the noble river, and glowing with the poetic nature of its Scottish author), as the boat glides upward from the sea, drink in its beauties, and live over again the strange history, the wild traditions, and quaint creations of fancy, that have made it famous throughout the world, and the voyage, seem like a dream of fairy land.

THE "VERMONT CENTRAL" is another powerful company, first-class in every particular, who lease all the roads running east, west and south through the New England States, up the lovely valley of the Connecticut to Lake Memphremagog and westward through the Green mountains to Burlington, where steamers are taken to the opposite shore.

WHITEHALL is at the head of Lake Champlain; 223 miles north of New York, 79 from Albany. As we break through the ledges and approach from the south, the valley spreads out toward the east in a fertile plain; at the right, toward the north, is quite a mountain, girded with outcropping ledges that run up from the east at an angle of about thirty degrees, and are broken off precipitously on the west; all along this front, houses cling one above another like rows of martins' boxes, and wooden stairways run zigzag up the sides, which, if bought by the acre, would bring the most measured perpendicularly while there would seem to be no difficulty at all in having a cellar right in the garret of a fourth story building. Climbing up the stairways we look down on the business portion of the village, close, compact and city-like below and thinning out gradually up the hill on the west. Going still higher, a pathway is found leading to the summit which is comparatively clear and affords a wonderfully fine mountain view for a very little exertion. From the south comes the canal and Wood creek, twin threads of silver twisting and turning; now at the east, now at the west side of the valley, cutting across in a succession of glistening loops. On the west are the mountains that separate us from Lake George; on the east, the level toward Castleton and beyond, the mountains of the island of New England — a thriving little dependency of the United States, separated from it by the Hudson river, Champlain lake and canal.

Whitehall was originally called Skeenesborough, after Col. Philip Skeene, who accompanied Abercrombie in 1758; was wounded in his attack on Ticonderoga and, after Amherst's victorious advance in the following year, was appointed commandant at Crown Point, at which time he projected the settlement. In 1765, he obtained a grant of the township and, in 1770, took up his residence here. On the breaking out of the Revolution he took sides with the Royalists, accompanied Burgoyne in his expedition against Ticonderoga and was captured with him at Saratoga; his property was confiscated by act of Legislature in 1779.

WOOD CREEK, that from its very head, has flown sleepily along, seems to have awakened suddenly and with a quick start, a joyous little run, a little foam and a little racket, plunges over the rocks, and dies out in the muddy lake at our feet. Close to the falls the canal boats and small steamers come, and line the banks of the bayou-like lake that leads away to the north through what seems a basin scooped out of the mountains, its marshy bed filled here and there with pieces of "made" land on which are steam mills, and long piles of lumber, which forms the principal business of the place. Through the marsh also runs the railroad to the landing beyond, where the large steamboats await the coming train.

FIDDLER'S ELBOW, where of old all the large steamers had to "warp" past, is a short, double crook, in the narrow channel, about one mile below Whitehall. Here rest the hulks of some of the vessels that engaged in the battle of Plattsburgh.

FORT PUTNAM is a high, rocky point, on the east side, where old Israel and his little band of Colonists lay in ambush for the French and Indians under Marin.

PUT'S ROCK, on the west side, is a flat, shelving ledge, running down to near the water's edge. Here it is said the old general once ran his horse off into the lake and escaped to the other side when pursued by Indians — vouched for by Whitehall generally. Close by is the dock where passengers and freight are transferred from rail to steamboat and *vice versa*.

BENSON, 13 miles from Whitehall, and Orwell, 7 miles further, are not particularly noticeable, unless it be for mud and the fact that they are on the Vermont side and that the boat touches there.

TICONDEROGA.

TICONDEROGA is 24 miles from Whitehall. Here are the ruins of the old fort, a good hotel and the place where the road from Leicester Junction joins the New York and Canada railroad, and where the fashionable route branches off over four miles of staging to the foot of Lake George, thence by steamer 34 miles to its head.

Here were enacted the principal events in the play of the lake; here savage tribes contended for the country on either hand; here three great nations struggled for the prize of a continent, and precious blood flowed like water for this, the key to the "gate of the country," by its position elected to become historic ground; as such, let us glance briefly in passing.

Claimed by the Hurons and Algonquins on the north, and the Five Nations, on the south, Lake Champlain was permanently occupied by neither, but the gateway between two sections that were continually at war with each other, the bloody middle ground over which each party in its turn swept carrying ruin in its path. This had driven all who would have occupied it beyond the mountains, and the lovely shores remained in unbroken solitude. Thus Champlain found it when, in July, 1609, he sailed south with the Indians from the St. Lawrence to make war upon their southern enemies, and "encountered a war party of the Iroquois on the 29th of the month, about ten o'clock at night, at the point of a cape which puts out into the lake on the west side." They each retired until the morning, when a battle ensued. Champlain was kept out of sight until they marched to the attack. He says: "Ours commenced, calling me in a loud voice, and, making way for me, opened in two and placed me at their head, marching about twenty paces in advance until I was within thirty paces of the enemy."

"The moment they saw me they halted, gazing at me and I at them. When I saw them preparing to shoot at us, I raised my arquebus, and aiming directly at one of the three chiefs, two of them fell to the ground by this shot, and one of their companions received a wound, of which he died afterward. I had put four balls in my arquebus. Ours, in witnessing a shot so favorable to them, set up such tremendous shouts that thunder could not have been heard; and yet there was no lack of arrows on one side and the other. The Iroquois were greatly astonished, seeing two men killed so instantaneously, notwithstanding they were provided with arrow-proof armor, woven of cotton-thread and wood. * * * They lost courage, took to flight, and abandoned the field and their fort, hiding themselves in the depths of the forests; whither pursuing them I killed some others. * * * The place where the battle was fought is 43 degrees some minutes latitude, and I named it Lake Champlain."* Ticonderoga is 43½ degrees north latitude and probably the cape referred to "which puts out into the lake on the west side."

The French claimed the country by virtue of Champlain's discovery, and in 1731, while at peace with Great Britain, they advanced to Crown Point and erected Fort St. Frederick.

The English claimed this territory by right of purchase and treaty with the Five Nations, and feeling that something must be done to prevent further encroachments of the French on British soil, General Johnson was sent, in 1755, to drive them away, going by way of Lake George, where he halted for a few days, when Baron Dieskau made a dash around French mountain, defeated Col. Williams' party and attacked the main army, in which he was defeated. He then returned to Ticonderoga and began the erection of a fort which he called "*Carillon.*"

---

* Documentary history of New York, see "Ticonderoga," page 32.

In 1757, it was occupied by Montcalm, who marched thence to the capture of Fort William Henry.

In 1758, Abercrombie made his unsuccessful attack on the old French lines, which resulted in his total defeat, with a loss of nearly 2,000 killed and wounded.

The following year Amherst entrenched before the lines, and the French, feeling that they could not successfully resist him, abandoned and set fire to the works, which the English took possession of in the morning. They then advanced on Fort St. Frederick, the French retreating down the lake; their hold on Champlain gone forever.

Amherst repaired and enlarged the works at Ticonderoga and Crown Point, on a scale of great magnificence, but never a shot from the frowning embrasures was directed against an approaching foe. Peace between the nations soon followed and the forts were allowed to fall into a state of ill repair and were poorly garrisoned when the revolution broke out. Crown Point had only a sergeant and 12 men and Ticonderoga 50 men all told, when in the gray of the morning of the 10th of May, 1775, Ethan Allen and 83 of his "Green Mountain boys," stole in through the wicket gate and demanded its surrender "in the name of the Great Jehovah and the Continental Congress." Crown Point was on the same day taken possession of by a party of Allen's men under Seth Warner, and soon after a sloop of war was captured by Benedict Arnold, by which the colonists gained command of the lake.

The following year Arnold, in command of a small flotilla, was defeated near the Four Brothers' islands by General Carlton, who advanced as far south as Crown Point, then retired into Canada.

In 1777 there came sweeping from the north the conceited, the pompous, the brilliant Burgoyne with 7,500 men and laid siege to Ticonderoga. St. Clair, then in command had barely sufficient troops to man the principal works, and when the English took possession of Mount Defiance, from which they could drop shot right over into the fort, he decided to abandon it and did so on the night of July 4th; all the stores that could be taken were removed, guns were spiked and at midnight a dusky throng moved away across the chain bridge. Unfortunately for the Americans, a house on Mount Independence was set on fire and the light revealed the fugitive army to the watchful enemy, who immediately pursued. The greater part retreated toward Castleton and were followed, engaged and beaten ; the English, however, suffered terribly, it is said, losing ten to one of the Yankees. The rest moving up the lake toward Whitehall were pursued by the British who broke through the chain bridge and reaching the head of the lake almost as soon as they, captured most of the stores and ammunition, the men retreating to Fort Ann ; after this Burgoyne moved south to Saratoga, where his march of triumph was changed to one of defeat, for he found the GATES too strong for him to pass.

After "Saratoga" the British retired into Canada, but in 1780 the old fort was again occupied by the troops under General Haldiman, at which time occurred those bloodless battles of diplomacy, where Arnold plotted treason with such consummate sagacity, that his country's enemies rested on their arms and " peace reigned throughout her borders."

Then came another enemy, silent, but resistless as the march of time. Rain and sunshine, frosts to rack and tempests to beat upon the old walls, until they totter and fall away, disappearing, one by one, and pointing to the time when naught shall remain but the name it bears, and that uncertain in the mists of the past.

"TICONDEROGA "*.— the generally accepted extract and boiled down result of over a dozen different Indian names, all, however, having something the same sound — as *Tienderoga, Cheonderoga* — meant to them the *coming together*, or *meeting of waters*,† instead of the generally accepted version of " Sounding waters."

CARILLON, the name given it by the French, meaning music, racket, a chime, may have been suggested by the " Sounding waters" near by.

The old battery on the bluff, at the steamboat landing, is

---

* For full description, with map of the ruins of to-day, see " TICONDEROGA."
† Colden, 1765. Pownell, 1774.

said to have been the original Carillon. Back on the higher ground are the barrack walls, trenches, two bastions and the best preserved portion of the ruins — a bomb-proof room, probably the magazine. On the east, by the east side of the road, is the old fort well. Leading from the south-east corner toward this, on the flat above, is the covered way, through which, it is said, Allen went in the gray of the morning, nearly a century ago. On the west is Mount Defiance; between it and the fort the outlet of Lake George joins Lake Champlain. Opposite the point to the south-east, the lake is narrowed down by the near approach of Mount Independence, which was also ortified when St. Clair had command there. Between the two points ran the chain or floating bridge. The lake now turns toward the north, thus washing three sides of the point. Up among the oaks, just beyond the tunnel, is the old French lines, reaching nearly across from shore to shore. Across the flat, where now stands a pleasant Hotel, lay Allen's route from the shore above, and it is probable, that near the railroad depot above, occurred Champlain battle in 1609.

The next landing is Larabees, on the Vermont shore, two miles distant.

CROWN POINT is nine miles farther, where the lake is sometimes left for Schroon lake and the lower Adirondacks, by way of Roots. A very good hotel stands here; the village is a mile further away.

CROWN POINT RUINS AND LIGHT-HOUSE is seven miles further on the west side, nearly met by Chimney Point approaching from the east; here the French erected *Fort St. Frederick* in 1731, the ruins of which may yet be seen on the shore, a little way north of the light-house; this soon became a noted trading port, where the Indians brought peltries to exchange for civilized whisky and other necessaries; the remains of lines of cellars, flagged walks, etc., testifying that at some time quite a village had stood there, it is said, with a population of 1,500. The extensive ruins further back are of the fort, commenced by Amherst in 1759. On the west is Bulwagga bay.

PORT HENRY — two miles from the Point, is noted for its

immense iron business and rich ore beds, found in the rugged mountains on the north and west; this is at present the northern terminus of the southern division N. Y. & C. railroad, but the work is being pushed steadily all along the west shore, and it is probable that soon an air-line railroad will connect the two great cities of the States and province.

WESTPORT is a pretty little village, on a deep bay, setting into the western shore, fifty-five miles north of Whitehall. This is the usual entrance to the mountain region by way of Elizabethtown, eight miles distant, thence to Keene; twelve miles farther. All through this region, west and south, the country is a succession of mountain and valley, or rather spurs and isolated peaks, around which flow the pleasant lower levels. (See page 131.)

THE ADIRONDACK SPRINGS, which of late are attracting considerable attention, are situated on the mountain slope, half a mile from the lake, midway between Westport and Port Henry. The springs are self-walled, with a substance something like that of the "high rock" at Saratoga; the depth varying from 10 to something over 18 feet, are owned by G. W. Spencer, who has accommodations for quite a number of guests, making it, with good fishing and sailing on the lake, a very pleasant retreat, whether in pursuit of health or pleasure. (See Index.)

Soon after leaving Westport, the spires of Vergennes, one of the oldest and littlest cities of the State, appear inland on the Vermont side, then the mouth of Otter creek, the largest stream in the State; here are the ruins of Fort Cassin, from which point, in the war of 1812, a lieutenant of that name repulsed the British flotilla, advancing to destroy the American ships on the stocks at Vergennes.

SPLIT ROCK.—Along the west shore runs Split Rock mountain, ending in the curious freak of nature, from which it received its name. Split Rock is a great, rough fragment of the mountain, containing, perhaps, a half acre of surface, nearly thirty feet in height, and separated from the main rock by a rift ten or twelve feet in width. Various theories are advanced, one of these that it is caused by the gradual attrition and disintegration of its asthenic particles by the combined dissilience of the elements, or some other cause, which is probably correct. Some say that this was of old the famous "Rock Reggio," so frequently mentioned in colonial records, and which tradition points out, first as the place where a great chief was drowned, from which it received its name; and second, as the boundary line between the Indians on the north and the Five Nations on the south. Watson claims, however, that Rock Dunder is the original "Rock Reggio," where the accident occurred. Either one is an easy thing to fall off of, if a body is so disposed.

Touching at ESSEX, a small village on the west shore, ten miles from Westport, the boat passes out into the broadening lake, gradually nearing the Vermont side in the approach to Burlington. Back, inland, are the two highest peaks of the Green Mountains, Mansfield, 4,350 feet above tide, and Camel's Hump, the *Leon Couchant* of the French. A prominent object, as we approach the city, is Rock Dunder, a sharp cone of rock 30 feet high. Farther out in the lake is Juniper island, and still farther the Four Brothers, where occurred Arnold's naval engagement with Carleton, resulting in the total defeat of the Americans. Away across, on the west shore, is Willsborough Point. Back of this the deep bay of the same name, a little way south is the mouth of the Boquet river.

## BURLINGTON.

Turning once more toward the east we behold, as we approach, one of the finest and most prosperous cities of the State, with a population of about 15,000. A long breakwater, with a light-house on each end, protects the shipping against the severe west wind. From the wharves, at the water line, the ground slopes upward, covered with lines of stately stores and dwellings, and appropriately enough overlooked by the University buildings of the State. It is 80 miles from Whitehall — a railroad center of considerable importance, and head-quarters of the Champlain Transportation Company. Here the Vermont Central railroad taps the lake, and tourists cross routes, going to the White Mountains and the Adirondacks, changing from boat to coach and coach to boat. There are two good hotels, the "American" and "Van Ness House," standing close together, and, as there is an active rivalry existing between them, they are naturally both first class. They are united on one question, however. All Vermont is. Earthquakes may rend this crust, and fanaticism turn man against his mother-in-law, but on one question Vermont stands firm. She venerates the hero of Ticonderoga— the leader of the Green Mountain boys—the Tell of Vermont— ETHAN ALLEN.—They vote for him to this day in the somewhat extended rural districts; they swear by him, and some who have learned of his decease are willing even to lie by him.

I saw him. I had a half day to spare, so approaching the affable (affable is a beautiful and appropriate title applied to all landlords now-a-days) proprietor of one of the hotels mentioned, I asked if there was any thing of interest about the city. He gazed at me a moment in astonishment, then, concluding that I was a foreigner, he casually mentioned a few hundred public buildings and parks, avenues, industries, individuals, etc.

"Any thing more?"

"Yes, sir. There's the statue of Ethan Allen, imported from Italy at a cost of several thousand dollars, and the marble column on which it stands, nearly 400 feet high "

"Je-ru-salem!"

"Yes, sir— the hill it stands on is 375 — then there are the lumber districts and market, the largest in the country, with one or two exceptions; lovely drives along the shore and out among the suburbs — to Boston, New York, Montreal and other places."

"Jupiter Tonans. Any thing else?"

"Yes, sir, situation sir; sit-u-a-tion. We think we lie the best of any city in the world — so natural and easy."

"Undoubtedly, sir, undoubtedly. I am amazed, astounded —any thing else?"

"Good Lord, Mr. a-a-a-what more *do* you want? Yes, sir, there is the University of Vermont, on the hill —' crowned by the University', the guide books have it — one of the grandest architectural triumphs of the *country* sir, *every*body should see it — it is *alone* worth a full day's inspection."

"Great St. Peter! Where is it?"

"I don't know exactly myself, but I can send a boy to show you the way, and I assure you, sir, that you cannot fail to admire it, it is imposing, sir, it is grand; I can personally vouch for that — excuse me, sir, here comes the Governor; here Johnny, trot this gentleman around."

PORT KENT, ten miles from Burlington, in a north-westerly direction, is not particularly noticeable, unless it be for its age, and it don't seem to take much pride in even that, it seems to have lost all interest in matters generally and is waiting for the time when the scream of the locomotive on the New York and Canada railroad shall be heard there, when it can gather up money enough to move away to some western country where it does not require so much work to gain a living; this does not apply to all the buildings, however, for along the brow of the hill are several very pleasant, comfortable looking houses, among them the old home of Elkanah Watson, whose account of travels in 1777, contain the best record we have of the towns and villages at that period. His descendants still occupy the homestead; his mantle, as historian falling on one well worthy to wear it, Winslow C. Watson, who has contributed much that is valuable to the annals of his native country and the valley of the Champlain.

We should have charity for Port Kent, however, perhaps it is worn out as it were, by the stages that come down from noisy Keeseville at all times of the day and night, storm or shine, to meet the boats as they touch at the venerable dock, "opposition, ten cents to Keeseville," or less if you consider that extortionate, and when the new plank-road is laid, which will be in operation soon, they will probably be willing to pay for your company. (See page 43.)

From Port Kent to Ausable Chasm, it is three miles, to Keeseville four. Just north of Port Kent is the widest, uninterrupted part of the lake. Three miles north of the landing on the west side is the sandy outlet of the Ausable river from which it is supposed to have received its name, Ausable meaning, literally, "a river of sand." A wooded depression in the ground above shows the course of the rapid river, but does not give indication of that wonderful chasm, "the walled banks of the Ausable," through which it foams and roars before its last quiet sinking away into the lake. Then we pass between Grand isle, belonging to Vermont, and the New York shore, past Valcour island, at the south end of which lies the "Royal Savage," sunk at the time of Arnold's battle with Carleton. Past Crab island, the burial place of the sailors and marines killed at the battle of Plattsburgh; and at last the pretty village itself, on the west side of Cumberland bay. North of this there is little to engage our attention, save the continued quiet scenery of cultivated shore and pleasant headland, at which we will hastily glance and return. We pass over the scene of the naval engagement, in 1814; round Cumberland head, three miles from Plattsburgh, and northward in the narrowed channel between the mainland and South Hero. Fifteen miles north of Plattsburgh is Isle La Motte; on which, at its north end, a fort was erected by the French in 1665.

On the east, between North Hero and Alburgh Tongue — the *Point Algonquin* of the French — an opening presents itself, the entrance to Mississquoi bay. Then 25 miles from Plattsburgh, 130 from Whitehall, we reach the northern terminus of the steamboat route.

ROUSE'S POINT. — The village is back to the south-west, a short distance, and not of very great importance; owing nearly all that it possesses to the railroad shops there and to its position on the border, where the custom-house officials rule with customary grace, and freight and passengers are transferred to boat and cars, going thence to the cardinal points of the compass. Here the trains on the Vermont Central cross over the long bridges and proceed westward toward Ogdensburg or north to Montreal. A little way north of the bridge is the fort commenced sometime in the past by the United States, and which will, from all appearances, be in ruins by the time it is completed. A mile further, a low belt of woods mark the boundary line between the States and Canada.

## PLATTSBURGH.

PLATTSBURGH is 105 miles from Whitehall; a flourishing village, occupying ground on both sides of the Saranac river. Has a population of about 8,000. It is of considerable commercial importance, being connected with Burlington and St. Albans by lines of ferries, beside the regular boats, and with Montreal by railroad, which also runs inland to Point of Rocks 20 miles distant. It has a number of fine stores, public buildings and elegant private residences. Just out of the village, on the south, are the remains of the earthworks occupied by the Americans in 1814, quite well preserved yet. The largest, Fort Moreau, in the center; Fort Brown, on the bank of the river, and Fort Scott, near the lake. About a mile south of the village are the old barracks, occupied occasionally during the late war by troops in training or preparing for the field; all the ruins illustrate too late a day in history, however, either to amount to much as antiquities, or take your breath away with suggestions of their former grandeur.

Plattsburgh deals quite extensively in lumber, fire-arms, historical associations and hotels, of which it has three worthy of notice, the Cumberland House and Witherill's, both large and inviting structures, situated in the business portion of the village, and Fouquet's, near the depot and steamboat landing on the lake shore, peculiarly a hotel for the tourist and summer travel generally.

FOUQUET'S HOTEL.

"FOUQUET'S HOTEL" has been a familiar sound to the traveling public for over seventy years, and the name alone carries with it assurance of excellence, rarely equaled in that line, needing no comment.

Their American progenitor came to this country with La Fayette, and, remaining, opened a public house in Albany. His son, John L. Fouquet, in 1798, erected a hotel near the site occupied by the present beautiful edifice. That building, being first class for that period, was burned during the siege of 1814 by hot shot from the fort. In 1815, a second house was erected on the same ground, with an improvement, both in style and dimensions. This, by repeated additions, had grown into a large and commodious establishment, but in June, 1864, it also was consumed. With an energy unsubdued by this calamity, the Messrs. D. L. Fouquet & Son commenced the erection of the third edifice, and the next year, on the same day in June in which the last had been burned, they opened a new hotel for the reception of guests.

## FOUQUET'S HOTEL.

The new building is an elegant and spacious structure, capable of accommodating one hundred and fifty guests. The rooms are large, well ventilated, and supplied with every thing promotive of comfort and enjoyment. The broad piazzas on two sides of the house, and the promenade upon the roof, afford a wide and delightful view of the lake, the battle ground and the scene of the naval engagement, the village, the surrounding country and the mountains on every side.

The second edifice flourished in the palmy times of traveling, when men journeyed at a rational speed to see and enjoy the country and the incidents of the road. Then the post coach occupied two days between Ogdensburg and Plattsburgh; but in the romance of the journey was the transit of the Chateaugay woods, along the government road, a distance of forty miles, through nearly an unbroken wilderness, where the traveler might frequently see deer gazing from the bushes, and occasionally a wolf prowling along the road. In those days, when a delicious, fresh salmon was in request, Fouquet had only to examine his net at the foot of the mill-race, or, that failing, to select a victim and spear him from a school beneath the lower bridge.

It was for many years the annual resort of General Scott, who made his home here for weeks at a time; and Capt. John B. Magruder, afterward confederate general, made his headquarters here, while his company was stationed at the neighboring barracks. At that time the old regimental mess of the First U. S. Artillery gave its dinners at the Fouquet House, to which British officers were often invited. Many legends are handed down of those jolly meetings, at which "Prince John" was the presiding and irrepressible genius.

The original name of this hotel was "The MacDonough House," named after the gallant naval officer of that name, who made his home here for a long time and was the personal friend of the first proprietor. The best likeness extant of the gallant hero is in possession of the present landlord.

Among the many officers who have been, from time to time, quartered here and lived at this house, we may mention the names of Wool, Bonneville, the gallant Hooker, Kearney and the genial Ricketts. Gen. Worth boarded here a long time and Stonewall Jackson was also a friend of the house. Of all these officers many characteristic anecdotes are yet current in the neighborhood.

The Fouquets were by nature and inclination hotel-keepers, and the present proprietor, L. M. Fouquet or " Lewie," as he is familiarly called, looks upon the calling as an art that has been and is to be his study through life. He is a polished gentleman, refined and courteous, with a large intellect; one of that nervous, high-strung nature, that do whatever they undertake with all their might, and sometimes his nervous fear that he has in some manner failed in doing all his duty, and his rapid skirmishing and flighty dashes from one thing to another verges on the ludicrous, until we realize that it is all for our benefit.

Flowers are a passion with him, his house seems like a great fragrant garden and the grounds animate with beauty and redolent with their odors; the best, indeed the popular, idea of the place, is of a train of dusty pilgrims entering a sweet bower and passing out refreshed — every lady bearing a huge bouquet "with Mr. Fouquet's compliments." His love for flowers is only exceeded by one thing, a mania for advertising, which he is free to admit is his besetting sin, and for the life of him he cannot yet decide whether it pays or not. Thousands of dollars have gone in all manner of ways to bring this house before the public in distant places, and foreigners think there is no way of getting into the United States except by way of Fouquet's Hotel, which is supposed to be situated in the midst of a vast tropical garden, where perennial sweetness reigns and embryo Nimrods sport. He is irrepressible; there is not the least doubt in the world, but that, cast away on some desert island at sunset, the morning would find it white with circulars containing directions as to the best way of reaching his hotel, and he seated in a bran new flower garden with a bouquet and his compliments in one hand for the first lady who should come along — engaged in an active correspondence with every railroad and steamboat company in existence, with the chances in his favor, that before night they would all be extending their lines toward his place.

Here our artist has drawn a plan of him, front elevation, taking the liberty that all great artists claim, of idealizing somewhat. The scene is laid in his garden, and the time — the exact moment when he is supposed to be making a floral offering to a lady — the compliments, of course, being understood, as they were too ethereal for the artist to grasp readily — in a cut of that size.

In the distance will be observed the summer-house and brick stable ; on the lake beyond, the battle of Plattsburgh is supposed to be raging, where, hid in its sulphurous smoke, the fleets of the brave Wellington and the invincible Farragut are engaged in deadly strife,— the facts were furnished by a newspaper correspondent, and this work of art will, without doubt, soon take its place beside the other great historical allegories at Washington.

Alas! time is flying and with it comes a sad thought — the last of his line and he a batchelor — let us draw the curtain, there is still some hope, but little encouragement. The future is a blank yet to be filled out ; the present a time to work ; the past has had its little bit of romance and is closed over forever.

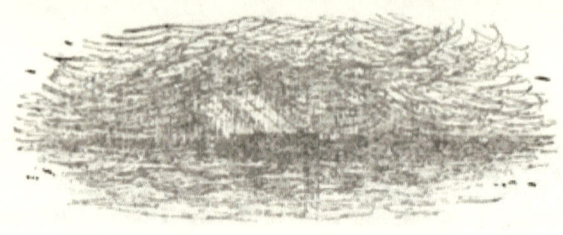

### THE BATTLE OF PLATTSBURGH.

It was a lovely morning in August, in 1492, when occurred the accident from which the village received its name. The glorious orb of day — the sun — cast his resplendent beams athwart the flower-decked bay, and was reflected back in glittering splendor from the myriad icicles that gemmed the pagoda on Cumberland head. Not a breath rippled the quiet bosom of the lake, as with swelling sails the Roman fleet swept around the point and bore down on the undismayed Turks, who stood their ground on the vasty deep like statues carved in living stone.

The attacking squadron, under Commodore Columbus, consisted of the flagship Santa Maria Smitha, the Mayflower, Captain Ben. Butler, the ram Ganouskie, and a large fleet of savage-looking canal boats. Of the above, the Mayflower, Capt. Butler, carried the most metal, also the largest bore; and although not belonging properly to that deal, had slipped in past the custom-house by connivance of an official, who had reason to feel grateful toward the commander.

The Greek fleet consisted of the Vermont, Minne-ha-ha — Hiawatha, commander; Adirondack, Oakes Ames and others.

"HOLT," thundered Commodore Inman, as the enemy cantered up:

> "Our Flagg is on the peak
> And we'll never Hulett down.
> While Columbia can squeak
> Anderson's can save the town.
> Rushlow down, Root — not rest,
> Bring the Grand Cannon, boys,
> We'll give them Babbitt's best.
> And never mind the Noyes."

Lurid lightning belched from the shivering flues; the ticking of a watch could not be heard in the battle's din; while the tottering air reeled beneath the fierce volume of tobacco smoke that tainted the fish for miles around, and covered the country so that scarcely an honest man could be seen in the legislature.

On shore the engagement was terrific. "My spoons! oh, my spoons!" shrieked Fouquet, as he saw the Mayflower round Cumberland House head; "Witherill I fly for safety? To horse, to horse; there are many pleasant drives around. Hang out the posters on the outer walls. Through tickets allow you to stop over. Martin to the front. Bartlett guard well the outlet. Pol swoop down on the enemy with your St. Regis braves like a moose on a sick punkie. Charge, men, charge. Put it in the bill; give them the devil—I mean the daffodil—with my compliments. To arms, to arms; man the breastworks; I'll not falter, though twenty times a batchelor."

Fiercely the battle raged; bravely they fought and well, until the quaking air was thick with glory and every tree sheltered its man. Oh, right glorious sight was it to behold the royal Africans as they rushed up, scenting the battle from afar. Oh, kingly joy to see the Vandal hosts swept as a wisp of smoke along the blackened plain. Mighty deeds were done, and individual instances of Jove-like courage leaked out in after years. A strange knight appeared suddenly on the field; whence, none knew. Some said from the hub of the universe, and wrought fearful slaughter with the long-bow, while his wild battle-cry rang out on the affrighted air: "Murraytotherescueaskjohn." The brilliant General Average was there and did nobly. Sheridan-twenty-miles-away waved his dripping decanter in the thickest of the fight, cheering the men onward, while General Major flashed everywhere. "If any one attempts to haul down the American bottle, shoot him on the spot," were the last words worth mentioning of the gallant Dix, as he fell badly wounded by a cold-water bombshell; he was cheerfully attended by Dr. Bixby, of the *Republican*, and, of course, never recovered.

Soon other reinforcements began to arrive. Fred. Averill's dragoons came in Harper & Tuft's four-horse coaches. Kellogg advanced from Long lake, and Martin came Moodily over from Tuppers. Old Mountain Phelps slid down into the enemy, creating a panic in the commissary department; while Mother Johnson turned such a fierce fire of hot pancakes toward them that they fell back in confusion, and when Bill Nye arrived with his mounted Amazons, they fled totally routed seeing which, the attacking fleet withdrew, badly riddled, the commodore's ship to discover America, the Mayflower only floating long enough to land its commander on Plymouth Rock, where he climbed into the gubernatorial chair and remained there until he was translated in a chariot of fire — which way the historian fails to state.

Thus ended this stupendous, double-headed battle, which gave liberty and the divine right of the franchise to four million Hottentots, and placed Plattsburgh on the same footing as the Declaration of Independence, and the glorious Fourth of July. Scream on, proud bird, scream on!

POSTSCRIPT, A. D. 1874.—An ancient manuscript, just brought to light, claims that the battle of Plattsburgh was fought on Sunday morning, September 11, 1814, Commodore Downie and Sir George Provost on the British side, against Commodore Macdonough and Gen. McComb on the American. It further states that the fleets were nearly equal, the position of the Americans about balancing the superior metal of the enemy, whose vessels struck their colors and surrendered one by one; the Americans, 3,000 strong, entrenched on shore, successfully beat back the 14,000 English, and caused them to retreat when night came. If there is any truth in this sensational account of the battle, the attacking party lost very heavily, which served them right for breaking the Sabbath.

There are many pleasant drives around Plattsburgh. Among them, one around Cumberland bay and one of especial interest south along the lake shore fording the Ausable river near its outlet, twelve miles distant, then passing up and through that grand freak of nature, the Ausable chasm.

CLINTON PRISON, at Dannemora, is 16 miles distant, and a very pleasant drive — when taken voluntarily. It is at an elevation of 1,700 feet above Plattsburgh; the ground sloping gently off into Lake Champlain and northward into the Canadas. Guides are furnished and visitors allowed to inspect the prison workshops and the ore-bed. They always have a number of people of leisure here, who, in this quiet retreat, pass their time in meditation, making shoes, cracking stone, etc. They are usually steady boarders and very select.

CHAZY LAKE is five miles farther, and noted for its trout, in which some find a peculiarly good flavor; they are taken in large quantities when found; it is about four miles long by one and a half broad, and has a comfortable hotel. Lion mountain is the highest point near by.

CHATEAUGAY LAKE is six miles west of Chazy lake, three by a rather rough road to Bradley pond, the balance a mere path. The upper lake is five miles long, by about two wide, with alternate sandy beach and rocky shores; there is a good summer hotel, a number of small boarding, and some very pretty private houses here, owned by "city folk;" three miles of winding stream toward the north, known as the narrows, leads into the lower lake, which is nearly the same length; it has a good hotel and a little steam yacht for the use of pleasure parties. From the outlet, it is eight miles over a comfortable carriage road to the railroad at Chateaugay. Seven miles from the outlet of the lower lake, the river is passing through a rift in the rocks, fifty feet deep, and very like that of Ausable Chasm, when it suddenly plunges off in an almost unbroken sheet as many more, then goes onward in a succession of rapids and cascades, between wild and broken walls, the scenery for a mile of its course being grand in the extreme; the foot of the fall can be reached through a ravine on the east; on the west side is a perpendicular wall of iron-stained rock; over the fall, the rocks on either side approach each other, and it is said that once a white man, pursued by the Indians, leaped across, while they, appearing on the other side, gazed down into the gulf and the water, flashing fifty feet below, declined to take the risk and allowed him to escape without further pursuit.

THE ARNOLD ORE BED, at Verona, three miles north of Point of Rocks, is a pleasant excursion, full of interest and instruction. It was discovered in 1806 by Stephen Baker, who, in crossing through the woods one day, discovered where a pine tree had been blown over, and in its fall torn up the earth around its roots, laying bare several yards of blue iron ore; he carried a piece to a blacksmith forge, and ascertained that it was of a very fine, tractile quality; being of small means, he "laid" with three others; one of them Elisha Arnold, afterward State Senator, who went on horseback to Albany, thence by sloop to New York, to Judge Winters, its owner, who, for $800, gave a deed of the land containing the bed; as Mr. Arnold left the house, he met a man who had been watching the iron finders for some time, and divining his object in coming here, followed him to New York, evidently in the hope of making something out of the information he had; in this he entirely failed; the mine was soon opened, and up to 1857 over 150,000 tons of ore had been raised; from that time it has had alternate times of rest and work, but since the railroad was built, has been in successful operation.

## CHAPTER III.

### NARRATIVE.

RING up the curtain to low, sweet music, the music of a September night, the blending of the myriad voices of the swamp into one long monotone, that seems to make you, wherever you stand and listen, its center. The scene is a dark waste of water, up out of which grow reeds and coarse grasses, that sway back and forth with the surging waves; over at the west is a low range of bluffs; on the east are mountains; near by, dusky white strips run here and there, beyond which a broader one reflects the cloudy sky, dark bodies are moving slowly along and lights twinkle as they pass to and fro; beyond, and to the south, a high hill rises up, belted with strings of stars; at its base they hang in clusters; they separate and pass up and down, are swung in circles, disappear and appear again in a most curious manner, and faintly comes the voices of the boatmen, the drivers, the lock-tenders, and the busy hum of the distant village. At the north, where the western wall comes down, the solid rock is notched out, over which rises the rocky crests of a mountain range, while away beyond winds the marsh-embordered rock-hemmed waters of Lake Champlain.

A low, rumbling sound comes from the south, then the solid wall that shuts us in on that side seems riven asunder, and from out the earth, with breath of flame, and eye of fire gleaming out ahead, thunders the night express. Across the marsh, it comes, bringing in its train a host of lesser lights, and with a shriek that clashes sharply and is broken into a confused din of echoes, it plunges into the northern wall, through the narrow cut to the other side, and with the hiss of escaping steam, the noisy clanging of its bell, the rattling of iron rods and links, the trembling, jerking and swaying of the long coaches, as the brakes are drawn hard against the moving wheels; then with the dying roar of its subsiding power, the iron monster rests at the end of its journey. Just for the moment we feel the hush.

" —— the rest of the tide between the ebb and the flow."

Then the nature of the sounds change, the quick, sharp words of command, of shouting and confusion, the shuffling of feet, as streams of life pour out from the various coaches, and converging, flow over the broad plank on to the boat that has been waiting to receive them; there is no need of asking the way; it is plain to all, for while on the left is nothing but darkness and a dingy, uninviting pile of buildings, on the right rises a great mass of white, with moving forms and flashing light; windows bright, with stained glass and frosted silver, rising tier on tier, begirt with beams and rods of iron, and above all, coming up from the fires below, wave banners of flame, whose fiery particles separating, dance away and are lost in the darkness. Whew! What a storm, not a thunder storm exactly, although there are indications of the sulphurous in the language sometimes heard, but a shower of baggage; it rains trunks, boxes, satchels, bundles, bags, from the car which has been brought to a stop directly in front of the gang-plank, and a double stream of trucks, drawn and propelled by stalwart men, go down under huge loads, and, coming up empty, run and wheel and dodge about, appearing always on the point of, but never actually getting run over.

Through all the confusion the man who seems to have the least to do stands quietly by the rail, seeing every thing, but saying nothing, unless occasionally to give a command in a low tone; then, as the last truck load is on the move, he touches a cord at his hand, a bell up in the pilot house tinkles, a few quick strokes on the big bell follows, the last man rushes over the plank, which is pulled aboard, and the great hawsers are cast off; then, again, the little bell, up where the pilot stands signifies that the boat is from thence out under his control, and he is responsible for her safety. Now, down along the wires to the engine-room the message goes; we hear the long hollow breathing of the steam as it rushes into the cylinder; the ponderous beam above tips slowly on its center; the wheels seem stepping on the water as they revolve; the great mass swings out into the channel, and moves away through the night like a great pearl surrounded by a luminous atmosphere. A little shining world all alone by itself.

Thus we saw it one night in the autumn of '73. *We* means the professor and myself. Who the professor is, or what he professes, doesn't matter, as long as this is a non-professional trip; but it may be of interest considering the field selected for our observations to know that the professor is not actually stupendous, either in length, breadth or thickness, and not particular about his diet; perish the thought! He simply abstains from the absorption of that mysterious compound known as hash, on account of the uncertainty of its origin. Revolts at sight of sausages, as it is unpleasantly suggestive of a dear little dog that he once loved. Can't endure cream in his coffee, because it "looks so, floating round on top," and whose heart bleeds and appetite vanishes if an unlucky fly chances to take a hot bath in his tea. To these peculiarities, add a disposition to see the fun in his own forlornness, and with boyishness dyed in the wool, the professor stands before you. As for the author of this, perhaps the least said the better. He hasn't the heart to say any thing bad, and a determination to confine himself strictly to facts, interferes somewhat with the glowing eulogy struggling to find vent;

suffice it to say, that nature was very lavish in the bestowal of longitude, although not noticeably so in regard to latitude, giving also a disposition to dare, and a physical development capable of enduring a vast amount of arduous rest. Going — the dainty professor and ease-loving writer, enthusiastic sportsman, with neither gun, rod, umbrella or other instrument of death, armed only with sketch and note-book, and hearts to drink in the glories of the great wild woods — to the mountains for health and strength to frames not over strong.

We found ourselves on board the "Vermont," the largest of the Champlain steamers; and as it swung out into the channel, went out forward, up odd little pieces of stairway and canvass side bills; ducked under and climbed over iron rods and groped along in the darkness on the hurricane deck to the pilot-house.

As we entered, our eyes becoming accustomed to the darkness, made out the form of Rockwell, the chief pilot, with two assistants, wrestling with the many-spoked wheel, which throbbed and trembled as they forced it over to one side, while the lights ahead seemed to swing swiftly past as we swept around a sharp bend in the channel.

A quick, low word of command, and the chain rattled and the wheel spun around like lightning as they jumped away from it.

"Now," said the pilot.

Six hands pattered on the polished spokes, and the air seemed full of clawing, jumping shadows.

"Over with her."

The wheel creaked and snapped with the strain brought to bear on it; the lights away out ahead, that had passed across to the right, now raced wildly back to the left, and we circled around in the darkness, out of which, into the circle of light that surrounded us, came reedy shores and low lines of bushes, seeming almost to brush against us as we passed.

"Steady now. Good evening, gentlemen."

The last half of the sentence, while it was friendly, was evidently intended as a sort of reconnoissance. It had inquiry in it, and said plainly, "I want to hear the sound of your voice."

## THE PILOT.    39

We said, "Good evening."

"Up a little — I know your voice — steady — let me see — let her run — Oh, yes; I remember now," and he greeted me cordially by name. "I saw you — hold her there — last summer. You came up here, and this other gentleman was with you. I didn't recognize your voice at first — hard over; that light's out again — you are a little hoarse; you ought to take something for that."

"We were; a trip to the mountains."

He said "it was an excellent plan to crowd her against the bank there let her chaw the re-action will clear her wished he could luff a point boys pass his life among the grand things hug the shore a little closer and look through nature up to nature's wind a little flawy, and she's down at the head. Then he sandwiched Beecher between Susan B. Anthony and Victoria C. Woodhull; said she was light aft, and clawed to starboard; asked if we could fully indorse Professor Tyndall's theory of nebular hegira; ruined the reputation of Andromedea and Cassiopia, and other heavenly bodies, by hopelessly entangling them with Butler and Massachusetts politics. Thought the Greek slave a perfect figure; said she sucked mud through here, sometimes, and they had to be careful of her flues. Wanted to know if we had given the evolement of solar faculae much thought; descended with Darwin to our remote progenitors; gyrated among the wheeling constellation; floated awhile through eternity; touched on the creation; paddled around with Noah; got lost with the children of Israel; skittered along down through the dark ages; said it wasn't going to rain; which suggested Sodom and Gomorrah and Lot's wife; wondered how many the Shah averaged, and thought he was no such man as the ridiculously proper Joseph. Admired Joan of Arc — said she carried an awful head of steam; but her boilers were good, undoubtedly, or Mr. Root would have made a fuss about it. Then he wanted our opinion as to the probable origin of creative energy and of the cohesive materialism of latent force. Shades of Egypt! the professor wilted, and we had to admit that Moses himself couldn't get us out of the scientific wilderness, and Rockwell thought Moses wasn't much of a pilot any way. And speaking of military men, he said "PHIL. SHERIDAN is a brick; just as full of fun as an egg of meat." He tells the following, which the general himself related when he, with the president and family, passed through the lake in 1872. They were at the "Thousand Islands," when one day Sheridan wandered off alone and came across an old farmer, with whom he entered into conversation, and ended by offering him a drink from his brandy flask. The old fellow took a generous draught; and, when pressed, even a second. Then, as the general was leaving, he suddenly bethought himself that he would like to know who it was that carried such good liquor. "Who be ye?" said he. "Who've I had the honor of drinking with?"

"My name's Sheridan," said the General. "No, be it though; ye ain't any relation to *General* Sheridan be ye?"

"Well, rather. *I'm* General Sheridan!"

"Ye *ain't though*," said the old farmer, who had a profound reverence for the hero of Winchester, whom he considered the greatest man living, hardly able to believe that he understood aright, "hev I been drinking with General Sheridan himself?"

"Yes, sir," said little Phil, pompously straightening up and enjoying the effects of his words, "you have had the honor of a drink out of General Philip Sheridan's own brandy flask."

The old chap gazed at the short, thick-set form before him, then a "sold" expression came over him, and his look of blended wonder and reverence changed to disgust, as he growled out, "Not—by—a—damn—site—little—feller—General—Sheridan's over—seven—feet—high."

Phil left, feeling that he had tried to pass himself off for a great man, and been caught in the act.

Thus, the pilot mixed art, science, physics and navigation, together; with an eye that never relaxed its vigilant watch out head, peering into the darkness, seeming to feel rather than see the channel; now shunning a dusky mass that proves to be solid shore when it comes within our circle of light, anon plunging into a deep abyss of darkness, apparently right into the mountain-side, whose shadowy form dances away as the eye seeks to fix its outline. Twisting about, now to the right, now to the left, now circling around a lamp hung out as a guide, then away toward others, that seem passing and repassing each other, as the boat sways to and fro, never touching, although, in places, a deviation the width of the boat to the right or left, would bring it on the muddy banks. Creeping onward through the night, at times seeming to hang out over the reeds, anon, waking a whole swarm of hissing, chuckling echoes, as we run close under a rocky wall; through the narrow west channel out across a dusky plane of light, to touch at a lonely looking dock; then onward, into broader strips of water and under the frowning promontory of Ticonderoga, then we went below.

Here, on the main deck, which on shore would be reception-room or general office, as the night advances, is to be found a motley gathering of all grades and degrees; some are doubled up to the seats which run along the sides and down through the middle, where, with mouths opened and hats tipped jauntily down over musical noses, they are enjoying a blissful repose; others indicate their right to wear bristles, by occupying two or three compartments of the same, and have worked themselves into a terrible chaotic state by limp attempts to accommodate their forms to the alternate soft cushions, and iron arms which separate them. Here lounges a jabbering group of laborers, probably destined to operate at some point on the New York and Canada railway, now being built along the west shore, and there on the floor, where it is necessary to step over or among them, to pass, is

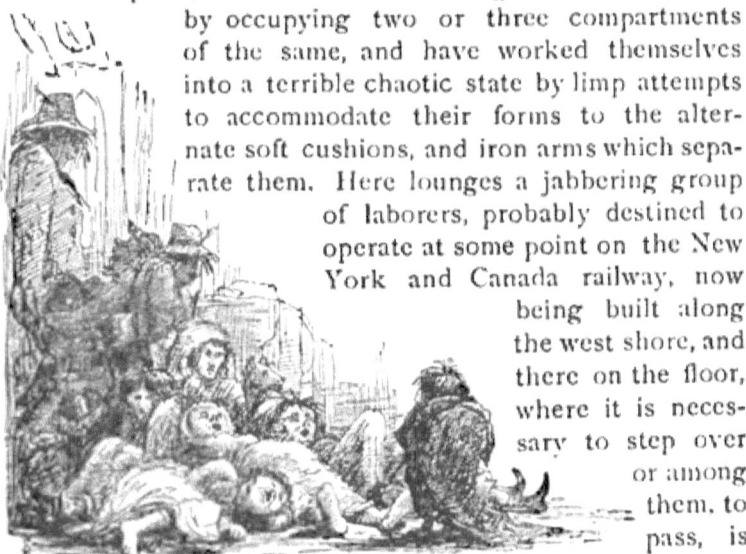

## "LO!" THE POOR INDIAN.

### (SHORTFELLOW.)

Should you ask me of this people,
Saying, who are these that gather
By themselves, and lying, slumber
In the night-time in the gang-way,
I should answer, I should tell you:

'Tis the children of the forest,
'Tis the mighty Indian nation,
Stealing, like the silent Arab,
Homeward,— for it is their nature,—
To their gracious queen's dominion,
From some giddy haunt of fashion
Where they pitched their birchen wigwam,
Made of hemlock boards and bed-quilts,
And "pursued the simple calling
Practiced by the gentle savage,"
Sleeping days, and nightly prowling
Where the laden clothes-line flappeth,
And the timid chicken roosteth.

See that untaught child of nature
With the proud and kingly bearing,
With a heart that knows not terror,
Wrap his raglan close around him.
Sleeps — and like an untamed porker,
Kicks and snorts in native freedom;
Heir to all the land about him
With the proof upon his person,
Fearing naught but soap and water
That might take his birthright from him.

See! the mother of her people
Sleeps the sleep of sweet contentment,
With her nose and toes upturning
And her native snore uprising
With its wild reverberations
Through the snags of yellow ivory
Like the winds of ocean raving
'Mong the reefs and crags chaotic
Of some wave-washed reeking cavern;
Or the wild tornado sweeping,
Through the lightning-riven hemlock;

See the dusky Indian maiden,
Graceful as the bending willow,
Sprawling 'round among the warriors,
Mingling with the dogs promiscuous,
With an air of free *abandon*
And of comfort, quite refreshing;
See! with modesty retiring,

From the rude gaze of the public,
They have drawn their scanty clothing
Close about their lovely faces,
Thus to hide their tender blushes.
*Length* we see was not essential
To the fashion of their garments;
*Not* voluminous their raiment
Nor elastic in its nature,
And in truth the pictured story
Is at least *unique* and novel,
For when drawn above their faces
It *must* lack in other places.

  Thus they gather, gather, gather;
In the night-time and the gang-way,
Old and young and middle-aged,
Squaw and Pappoose, Dog and warrior,
Interlaced and intermingled
Like the fish-worms in a bait-box,
Human hash of doubtful gender,
Dream of chaos, radiating
Legs and arms and sounds mysterious,
Odors earthly and of spirits,
Come of contact with the pale-face.

  Lo! the poor but honest Ingin,
With his dark eye full of sadness,
Full of rayless, hopeless longing,
Gazing backward, ever backward
To that happy time now vanished,
When he wandered o'er the prairie,
O'er the mountain and the fenland,
Through the dark and tangled wildwood,
Free as bird or winds of ocean
Or the scurrying mists of cloudland,
Drifting, drifting, flitting, passing
Out upon that boundless ocean,
To the unknown, the hereafter,
Vanishing before the pale-face,
Melting like the fleeting sour-
Kraut before a famished Dutchman.
  *Sic transit gloria mundi*
  *Hinc illæ lacrymæ.*

Jupiter was high up in the east, shining like a young moon, and faint signs of coming day were apparent when we left the steamer, and passing into the shadow of that architectural triumph on the dock at Port Kent, got into the waiting stage and set out for Keeseville. Climbing the hill a ride of three miles over what we took to be a "corderoy," but which we were informed was the remains of a plank-road, brought us to Birmingham Falls at the head of Ausable Chasm; here the professor and I alighted on the steps of the hotel while the stage proceeded on its way to Keeseville, a little more than a mile distant.

The CHASM HOUSE is one of those large comfortable looking old stone houses with generous apartments, great roomy window seats and an air of substantial home comfort about it not often found in hotels; it was built for a private residence and altered over to accommodate travelers when the growing interest felt in the Chasm demanded a place of entertainment, having accommodations for about 20 guests, and is a very pleasant quiet place to stop at. The proprietor H. H. Bromley, is a jolly, easy-going sort of fellow, ever ready to devote himself to his guests, not seeming to own himself when they are around, and withal a pleasant companion on the various excursions to be taken from his house. Soon a shuffling sound was heard within, a light appeared in the hall, the door was thrown open, and there, with hair awry, one eye half open, and arrayed in a partially adjusted pair of pants, with wonder on his phiz and a lamp in his hand, stood the proprietor. "Well-by-thunder," he remarked by way of greeting, recognizing one of his visitors; then his six-foot-form assumed the appearance of a wet rag as he dropped back and apparently hung himself up against the door-post while he went through the form of an ecstatic laugh without the slightest sound escaping his lips. We couldn't see any thing funny, and I don't think he had the least particle of an idea of what he was laughing at, but he seemed to drop off into a laugh, simply because it required less exertion than to keep sober. Then we went inside, our host foraged around for pillows and blankets and retired to his bed once more, while we curled down on a pair of sofas, getting another night's rest and rising refreshed to partake of a late breakfast and to do the wonderful Ausable Chasm.

"WELL-BY-THUNDER."

AUSABLE CHASM.

## CHAPTER IV.

#### AUSABLE CHASM.

A LITTLE depression in the otherwise level country, a wooded valley with gently sloping sides, marks the site of this grand wonder — a Yosemite in miniature almost at the doors of the great city, and curiously enough, comparatively unknown. The river flowing quietly along the valley from the south and west, passes Keeseville, plunges over Alice Falls, square against a solid wall of rock, turns at right angles and, wheeling around in confused swirls, now right, now left, falls in a mass of foam over the rocks at Birmingham, then hurrying downward between towering cliffs and over rocks where the sun never shines, emerges from the gloom out into the glorious sunlight, and onward to mingle with the muddy waters of Lake Champlain.

This freak of nature is not alone of its kind, but one of a system of rents in the earth's surface that probably extend all over the northern portion of the State, the most noticeable of the others being at Chateaugay Falls; on the Opalescent, and higher up on the east and west branches of the Ausable. Neither are we to say how or when they were formed; the walls that now are from ten to fifty feet apart, were undoubtedly sometime united and solid; projections on the one hand are often faced by corresponding depressions on the other; layers of rock on one side duplicated on the other. Prof. Emmons, State geologist, found here petrified specimens of the lowest or first orders of animal life, and ripple marks made when the rock was in its plastic state; above these in successive layers, towers seventy feet of solid rock.

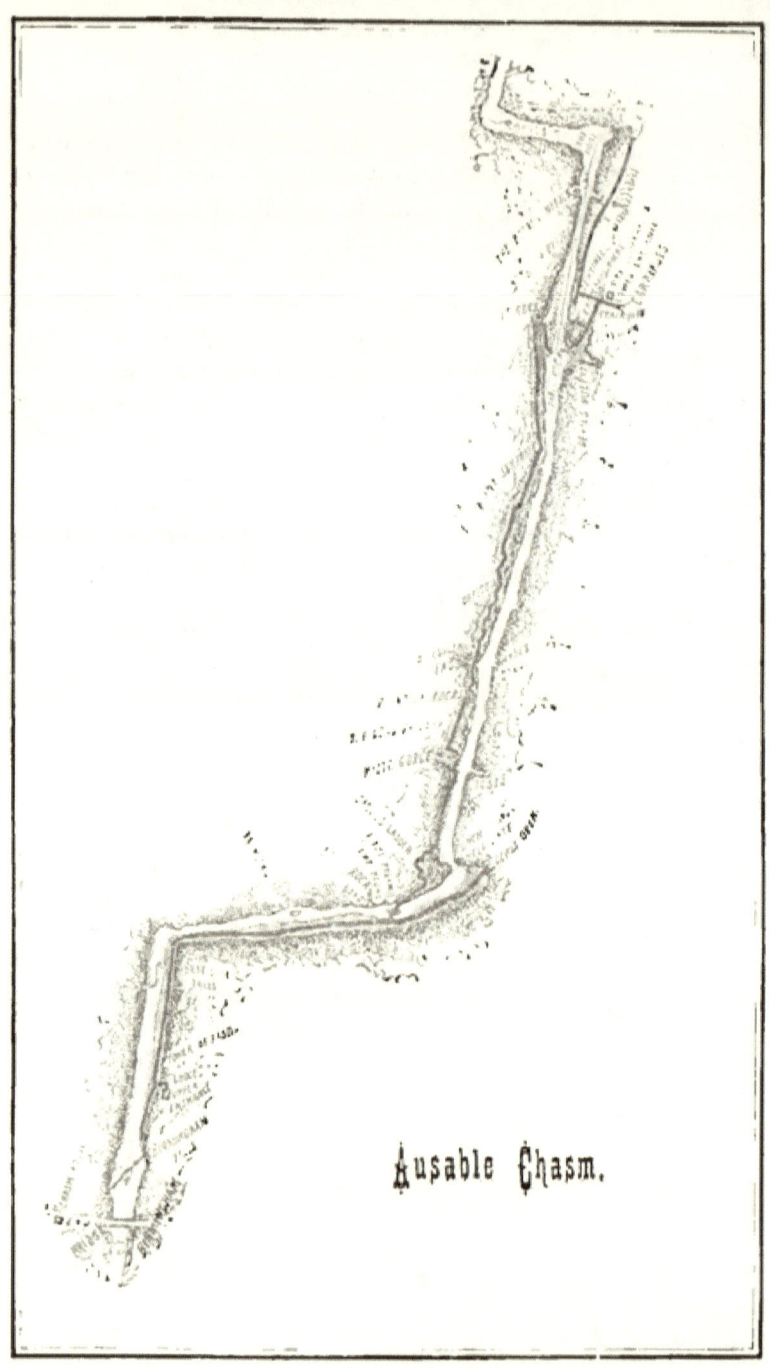

## AUSABLE CHASM.     47

Who can say what ages have passed away since the restless sea beat upon that unknown shore and left the mark of its wavelets for us to wonder at, thought is lost away back in the eternity of "the beginning," when darkness was upon the face of the deep, then came the dawn of creation and in its full light the lowest of animal creatures lived their brief day and added their mite to the ocean's bottom, which was gradually lifted above the surface, and drying, cracked as we sometimes see clay in the road, sun dried after a summer's shower. Time came and went, long ages rolled away and floods swept over the uneasy world that reeled and staggered under the pulsation of its mighty heart of fire; in places the thin shell bubbled up into mountain ridges, and breaking, cooled; then came the glacial period when great ice-bergs passed across, grinding uplifted points to atoms, and, carrying huge boulders onward in their course, dropped them miles from where they were taken; then the waters fled away, the seams and cracks were filled with the rich alluvium, holding in its bosom the germs of vegetable life that in time covered the world with a mantle of beauty. The yearly rains descended, the waters from the mountains swept downward through the valleys, carrying all before them, the loose deposit that once filled the walled banks of the Ausable, floated outward into Lake Champlain, and left revealed the main artery in this wonderful network of rifted rock.

Until recently there had been but little done to open the chasm to the comfortable inspection of the public. Some parts had probably never been visited, and there were but two or three places where it was considered safe to climb down into the gorge. However, in 1873, a company of Philadelphians secured nearly all the land surrounding, have commenced the erection of a hotel near by, and built stairways, galleries and bridges so that nearly the entire length can now be traversed with comfort, the remainder in a boat.

Passing through the "Lodge"— the Professor, Bromley and I — and descending by a stairway of 125 steps to the bottom, we passed up into the spray from the cataract, which, divided in the center, falls in almost unbroken sheets a distance of seventy feet, hurries northward to the Horseshoe Falls, passing over which it butts squarely against the wall at the Elbow, and turning to the east goes swiftly onward in its narrow, tortuous channel.

BIRMINGHAM FALLS.

The cave known as the "Devil's Oven" is a hole in the rock about thirty feet deep by twenty high, which we entered, feeling that it would do no harm to get accustomed to the thing, as there is a good deal of uncertainty concerning the future. We found it much more comfortable than the name would lead one to expect; and here let me remark that his majesty seems to own considerable real estate in the neighborhood, claiming, beside the "Oven," a "Pulpit," "Easy Chair," "Anvil," "Stairway" and, of *course*, a "Punch Bowl." Here, at the left, the waters break through "Hell Gate," into the eddy called the "Punch Bowl." Just above the "Oven" a light bridge is thrown across the foaming torrent and a set of nearly one hundred steps lead zig-zag up over the point and down on the other side, then along a gallery to the bridge of the "Mystic Gorge," a *crevasse* leading off at right angles with the main fissure toward the north and continued in a similar opening on the south.

"MOSES."

"What is that called?" said we, alluding to a huge rock that towered up almost over our heads, across the Chasm. Bromley scratched his head and regretted that he had been unable to find a name for it yet. Poor fellow! he has done well, and already shows signs of approaching baldness, caused by frequent attempts to dig out appropriate and nice sounding names for the many objects of interest near by. "Call it Moses," suggested the Professor, and "Moses" it was christened by unanimous consent. "Who was Moses?" The question was asked soberly, and a quiet individual who had joined us, with a book in his hand and a semi-ministerial hang to his clothes, proceeded to tell us in good faith, as he supposed the question was asked by an anxious inquirer after knowledge. How insignificant we felt looking up at the strip of blue sky, the great river walls and the dark tower of rocks above us—"henceforth shall you be called Moses; fit emblem of thy namesake who stood face to face with the great Creator amidst the thunderings of Mount Sinai."

A little further on the gallery runs along half way up the almost perpendicular side of the Chasm, around "Point of Rocks" to the "Smugglers' Pass" nearly opposite which is "Howe's Cave," along past the Post-office, suggested by the honeycombed rock at the side showing deposits made by the water in times of floods thirty feet above its present level, then over and down on "Table Rock." Here they end, and stepping into a boat we can be set over—we can almost jump across—and stand under the "Sentinel" and "Cathedral Rocks."

CATHEDRAL ROCKS.

Now for some ways down (I could not judge of the distance, for the senses seemed overwhelmed with the grandeur of the scene) the water runs straight away, shut in by walls reaching perpendicularly up, and so near together that it seems as though you could almost leap across from one to the other, then turns squarely again toward the north. We stepped into the little flat-bottomed boats, and Bromley, seizing the paddle like the grim ferryman of the Styx, with one of his silent though hearty laughs pushed out into the stream. The swift water caught us and we were whirled onward, under the great walls, and carried swiftly down the stream. Once, where the water scooped downward over a rock and then curled over, as if trying to climb backward upon itself, it came in over the sides, wetting us slightly, but we passed onward into the lower gateway, where the water piled up in the centre, and lifted us like cork on molten lead, then out into the eddy under the protecting point, whence we climbed up out of the depths to the surface of the earth, glad to get out into the clear sunlight once more. We had left the world above, descended to Hell Gate, cooled off in the Devils Oven, ascended and descended Jacob's Ladder in any thing but an Angelic state of perspiration, moralized over Moses, wondered what mystery there was about the mystic gorge, scrambled mildly past Point Surprise, gazed reverently up at the Devil's pulpit, ran the Sentinel, and after a tempestuous voyage in a gallant scow, effected a masterly landing, and were glad to get out, for while we felt that it was good to be there where we realized our own insignificance, it came to be oppressive at last, and we felt with Will Carlton that

"To appreciate heaven, well
It is good for a man to have some fifteen minutes of hell."

If unwilling to take the boat ride, which is ordinarily perfectly safe, you can ascend the old stairway in Cathedral Rocks to the level above where the carriages meet those who do not wish to return through the Chasm and where refreshments can be procured if desired.

Here and at the "Lodge" entrance also, will be found photographs of the many points of interest throughout the Chasm, among them, many that are actually works of art. The kind universally acknowledged best are known as the "Crystal," and sold at $2.50 per dozen; next are those published by Purveyance, which are excellent although lacking the needle-like sharpness and delicacy of the former. W. G. Baldwin at Keeseville is general agent for all kinds, and his rooms at that place are well worth a visit. (See catalogue of views on page 197.)

### KEESEVILLE.

At Keeseville we dropped in on our genial, eccentric old friend Lansing, of the *Republican*, for information ; because editors know all about every thing, and as they don't have to work it relieves the monotony of their idle life, by allowing them to contribute something for the benefit of anxious seekers after knowledge — we were made happy. Keeseville is situated on the Ausable river, about five miles from its mouth and is a thoroughly wide-awake little village, not set upon a hill, actually, but rather the reverse, and a person wading across the sandy plain on either side will be surprised when he reaches the front of the hill to see so much life and business in the hollow below. The water-power is immense, and utilized by the twine, wire and horse-nail manufacturers — the latter being the principal industry of the town. There are also several elegant private residences, churches and stores, built of Potsdam sandstone, which here abounds.

AUSABLE HOUSE.

The Ausable House is kept by E. Averil, who, although young in the business, keeps an exceptionally good hotel, and has earned for himself a host of friends among the pleasure seeking public. The house will accommodate nearly a hundred guests, the rooms large, with high ceilings, nicely furnished throughout, beds good, table well supplied, and what is considered, by some, better than this even, always clean, fresh and attractive. See page 167.

Connected with the house is the well kept livery of Harper & Tufts, veteran stagers both, who run lines in all directions centering in Keeseville; meeting the boats both day and night at Port Kent, the trains on the N. Y. & Canada Railroad at

Peru, and up along the Ausable river to the Saranac Lakes via Whiteface Mountain and Wilmington notch when desired. See routes, page 156.

The Ausable Horse Nail Co. was organized in 1862 with a capital stock of $80,000. Now, the shares are valued at fabulous prices, due, it would seem, to the company's possession of the right to use the little machines by which the nails are shaped, the invention of Daniel Dodge, who unlike most inventors, has made money out of it. Here they have over 50 of the little machines in operation, capable of turning out 150 pounds each, finished nails per day, 100 nails to the pound, and worth, on an average, 24 cents per pound.

One firm, that of W. Mould & Son, deserves especial notice for their Yankee push and enterprise. The elder member of the firm has long been a moving power in every scheme of progress started in the village, and his presence is felt in many places where his name does not appear. Their store is a wonder in its way, a curious mixture of city elegance and country heterogeneousness; there are found railroad tickets and perfumery, periodicals and prescriptions, real estate and fishing tackle, black-fly ointment and works of art. In the same building is Baldwin's photograph store, where will be found the largest collection of photographs, large and small, of the Ausable Chasm, and the Adirondack region in general, north of New York, which may be of interest to some in these days when everybody is " making a book " of views.

THE NAIL-ROD WORKS — On the road between Keeseville and the Chasm, are also well worth a visit. See that mass of iron as it is brought from the furnace door, glowing with heat, scintillating and spluttering like a young fourth of July; the tongs which grasp this lump of fire are suspended by a chain from a wheel which runs along the iron track over head. Now it is swung around under the great trip-hammer which descends, softly at first then swifter as the glowing loop shrinks down weeping tears of blood. Another heat and it is passed through between iron rollers having grooves of various sizes running around, through the largest first, then a size smaller, and this repeated until it gets too cold to work or is as required.

Once more they come from the furnaces, glowing red, and as the flat bars pass through the last set of rollers it comes forth nearly round. Now it is passed rapidly through, back and forth, each time lengthening out farther than before, and as it is constantly forced along it writhes and squirms about on the black floor like a serpent of fire — a string of red hot iron seventy to eighty feet in length. This is nail rod. Now cut in convenient lengths it is passed to the several workmen, who, heating it in small furnaces, feed it to the curious little machines in front of them, which, eating red-hot iron, drop finished nails like the ticking of a watch.

Leaving Keeseville, our road followed along up the valley of the Ausable, through a fertile farming country, that gradually gave place to a wilder and more broken district, while the river grew rapid and the hills along its shore became rocky and precipitous. Clintonville, with its said-to-be largest forge on the continent, and decayed, ashy, sooty look, was passed as was "Point-of-Rocks," the southern terminus of the Plattsburgh Railroad. At Ausable Forks (which also bore unmistakable signs of being a coal-handling town) we left the regular stage route, and climbing to a sandy plateau west of the village, picked our way through a forest of stunted pines, choosing our road from a multitude that seemed to cover and run in every direction across it. Three miles of this sandy way through the woods and we came out on the western slope, in full view of the towering form of "Old Whiteface," and — through Wilmington Notch — the blue of the more distant ranges. Then down in the valley we went, and up along the rapid Ausable to where we strike the stage road once more, having saved over two miles by our cut through the woods. Our driver seemed much interested in mill privileges, talking *dam* to his horses a good share of the time; and when we inquired if he was a christian he dodged the question and remarked something about a dam in California. Then he pointed out the ruins of an old forge and said somebody dammed the river there once; this horrified the Professor, but he soon recovered sufficiently to intimate that it didn't look worth a dam to him, and thought that if it was true it was dammed bad.

At last we entered the little hamlet of Wilmington and drew up in front of the hotel — not a very elegant affair, to be sure, but we felt at home as soon as we caught sight of the big, honest, square-looking fellow with his pants in his boots and fun in his clear blue eye, who came out to meet us. We inquired if he was landlord.

"Well, I don't know," said he, with a glance down at his working clothes; "it's been so long since we had any company that it don't pay to keep a landlord." Then he continued sadly: "The season's about over, I guess, for you're the first travelers we've seen in a week." Then he took us inside, built up a rousing fire, and in a short time gave us a dinner that could not fail to satisfy the most fastidious.

THE WHITEFACE MOUNTAIN HOUSE is a comfortable looking two story building, with a double piazza running along the front and side toward the mountain from whence it derives its name, and has accommodations for about fifty guests. It is on the east side of the Ausable river, which is here quite narrow. On the west the land slopes upward for a short distance then rises rapidly, sweeping away with but one or two breaks to the summit of "Old Whiteface."

Wilmington, aside from the hotel, has a deserted, worn-out sort of look, and while it appears to possess a little of every thing it seems as though nothing ever came to a head. Two or three shut-up-looking stores, three shut-up-looking churches — Methodist, Presbyterian and Lutheran — a few scattering houses, an old forge, saw, starch and grist mills, all having a decidedly dead appearance. The place was owned a long time ago by one Major Sanford, who came here, built two or three stills, and went to making whisky. "Those were the times when it wasn't a sin to make it; they didn't put in as much poison as they do now-a-days," said my informant. "Well, he went to making whisky, built mills and that brick church and then failed. Then George Weston came here with $10,000, cut a road to the top of the mountain and built a little house up there; but he soon lost all *his* money and sold out to Sidney Weston of Winooskie, Vermont, who is smart as lightning and will make it pay if any living man can."

SUMMIT OF WHITEFACE MOUNTAIN.

## CHAPTER V.

### OLD WHITEFACE.

UT off from its kindred on the south by Wilmington Notch, and on the north by one almost as deep, pyramidal in form, although somewhat the longest north and south, its base clothed in inky spruce and balsams, its naked granite head among the clouds "Old Whiteface" stands one of the finest mountain peaks in the Adirondacks.

"I'll tell you what I'll do," said our warm-hearted landlord at night as we sat discussing *pro* and *con* the ascent of "Old Whiteface," "if you will stay over I will take you two miles up the mountain — as far as we can conveniently get with a wagon — and send a guide to the top with you, for it's the grandest mountain view to be had in the Adirondacks, and I don't want you to go away without seeing it." Of course we accepted, only insisting that he go with us. So at nine in the morning, with the thermometer at 48, we set out up the mountains; we left the wagon which returned to the hotel, with instructions to meet us at sunset, and proceeded up the bridle path toward the summit, traveling about a mile westerly then turning toward the south, entered the standing timber and began the ascent in earnest.

At the end of a half hour we had gone another mile and came out on an open space called "Lookout Point," half way to the summit. Here the blueberries grew thick, and we scraped whole handfuls from the bushes and ate them — in ten minutes gathering all we cared for. Then we resumed our course and pressed upward through the dark woods, scrambling up the steep path where great rocks alternated with pools of black muck in a semi-liquid state, trodden and mixed by horses' feet, and we wondered that horses could climb such places with a hundred and fifty to two hundred pounds of humanity on their back; but Baldwin said to his knowledge not an accident further than being lost for a night, ever happened on the mountain. We reached the shanty, three-fourths of a mile from the summit, a little past noon, and here occurred a desperate encounter between three men on the one side and six slices of bread and butter, supported by other fixtures, on the other, which resulted in their total defeat and destruction.

The shanty is in a small clearing, at the highest point where wood and water can be obtained, has log sides, with a roof, part canvass, part bark. Within is a parlor and cook stove; along one side, raised a little above the floor, a platform that looked as though it might do service as Brigham Young's family bedstead, was covered with spruce and hemlock branches, and blankets. A sort of cross between a stairway and ladder led up to the ladies' dormitory under the sharp roof, through which the stars could peep in places. Here, in the bed which was over nearly the entire floor, "permiscus like," we could discover signs of the tender feeling with which the fair sex was regarded — in the springy moss and fine leaves which had been stripped from the hemlock branches, on which the lords of creation slept down below. The pipe from the stove in the lower room, where a fire can be kept roaring all night, passed up through this one, and altogether it was a cosy, jolly, fun-provoking place to be in, where, as our guide remarked, " if there was any fun in a fellow it was going to show itself." We, in imitation of others before us who had written their names in every conceivable and reachable place in the building, registered and proceeded on our way to the summit.

" Pretty rough work," said Baldwin, " but hundreds of people come up every year and ride clear to the top. A big doctor came here from Buffalo with his family and a four-horse team that he had been all over the country with — a very valuable team, too, — and when he said he was going to the top of the mountain with them I tried to stop him, and I offered to get horses that were accustomed to the road for nothing, rather than have him hurt his, but no; 'other horses have been there, have they not?' said he, and when I told him yes, he said, 'then mine can go;' so he took them out of the harness and put his wife, a woman that would weigh two hundred, on the firiest one of the lot and started, and I felt bad for I knew something would happen, and they rode those horses to the very top and just turned around and " ——. We gazed down over the fearful precipice at our feet while our hearts seemed to cease their motion as he slowly concluded — " and rode down again without getting a scratch !"

"But how can ladies manage to keep on the horses' backs, where it seems almost impossible for the horse to get along alone?"

"*Manage!*" said he, "like a man, of course, astride, and it makes me laugh to see them sometimes when they find that they've got to go in that way. So modest when they start, some of them, that they are dreadfully afraid of showing their *feet*, but they soon get over that and come down with colors flying. I don't know as they would ever have done it if Mrs. Murray, wife of the Rev. Adirondack Murray, hadn't set the fashion herself. She's a dashing, independent sort of woman, who don't let thoughts of what people may say interfere with her plans. Well, after Mrs. Murray set the example, we had no difficulty, and now lots of them go up in that way; as, with the horses we have and a guide at their sides, there is not the slightest danger in making the ascent." The regular price for a horse and guide is six dollars, or four dollars for the horse alone; but unless a lady is perfectly at home in the saddle, she will be apt to wish she was "at home" in reality. It is needless to add that the Turkish costume is considered the most appropriate for this style of amusement.

All the way up we had noticed fresh tracks made by three several persons — one, a man's, which also appeared to have descended, and two evidently made by ladies — one short and thick, the other slender and dainty in its manner of touching the ground. It had been a matter of wonderment to us, and "Little Foot-prints," as we styled the owner of the dainty stepping foot, was a constantly recurring subject of speculation. "Where is Little Foot-prints? who is she? is she pretty? — of course. And the other — why are they apparently alone, when the Big Foot has gone back?" questions that we hoped soon to solve; questions that preyed upon the Professor, as the oft-twirled moustache and passage of his fingers through his auburn locks would seem to indicate. Of course it was nothing to me, and only out of mere curiosity that I managed to reach the top first, but "where was Little Foot-prints?" Not there, certainly, for the summit, the sides and the backbone of the mountain up over which we had passed were primeval, unyielding rock. They had not returned by the path; they might have plunged down the sides in some other direction, but the feeling took possession of us that our "Little Foot-prints" had taken wings and flown up among the angels, just a little higher than where we stood.

How can I describe it — the wonderful beauty of the day, the clear, crisp atmosphere surrounding us — the great purple-rimmed basin, in the center of which, lifted up on a pinnacle, we stood, while the mighty, sweeping dome of heaven came down all around and blended with the mountain edges. A keen, wintry blast sweeping past, penetrating even through the heavy blankets that we had brought from the house below; the bits of ground frozen nearly as hard as the rock on which they rested; every stunted bush and blade of coarse grass which clung to the wind-swept summit gleaming with frost needles and sparkling like spun glass in the bright sunshine; while below, the country lay spread out in the glory of its autumnal dress, its gold and crimson, brown and green, its pearly lakes and threads of silver, its purple hills and mellow distance, over which lay a mantle of tender blue haze, seen only in autumn — not smoke — but something that suggests the thought of the myriad millions of pale, sweet ghosts of falling leaves and dying flowers. Back toward the north ran the sharp ridge up which we had toiled, naked and dark for a quarter of a mile, then a stunted growth of balsams gnarled and twisted; a few live branches low down at the surface, the tops dead and dry; then, as we look further the spruce and cedar grow dark and thick down to the belts of birches and maples below. Away off to the east is Lake Champlain, lost in the mist toward the north, shut in by the Green Mountains, and beyond, the white hills of old New England. To the south lay the great peaks of the Adirondacks. "Haystack,' "Marcy" — the cloud-piercer of the Indians, "Colden," with the white track of the avalanche down its side, and others — a long line of giants, their dark blue crests rising like ocean billows — grand and changeless in their mighty forms, overwhelming in their sublimity.

Away toward the west a lower set of mountain waves are seen, over a comparatively level tract of country cut and outlined with a confused network of ponds and streams, with here and there a broad, shining sheet of water; Lake Placid at our feet, the Saranacs and Big Tupper's farther away, and a host of others, too numerous to mention, while over the purple rocky rim of the mountains to the north stretched the faint blue of the level Canadas, through which was the silvery gleam of the mighty St. Lawrence.

Turning once more toward the grand Indian pass we see the fields of North Elba, and — a mere speck — the home and resting-place of old John Brown. From the pass above, the Ausable rises and comes toward us; here and there we catch glimpses of it, a mere thread, through Wilmington Notch, under the great wall, through the natural flume at our feet, past the little village and away to Keeseville beyond which it plunges down over the rocks at Birmingham, and finds its way out through the dark chasm to Lake Champlain.

Seventy years ago an avalanche of loose stones and the gathered moss and vegetable deposit of ages went down the western slope of this mountain and the exposed surface, whiter than the rest, is said to have given it the name; but there is a more reasonable theory, as the line can hardly be noticed unless covered with snow, that the old giant's naked brow, for so long a period covered with snow, suggested the name of " Old Whiteface." On the topmost point, firmly attached to the rock, we found the card of the chief of the Adirondack Survey, a metallic disk with this inscription : " Whiteface Mountain, Station No. 2. Verplanck Colvin, S. N. Y. Adirondack Survey, 1872." All around, the surface of the rock was scarred and chiseled with the names of former visitors while on one, cut deep and clear, were the words,

"Thanks be to God for the mountains!"

and every heart joined with that grand old mountain peak in saying, " thanks be to God for the mountains." A great, dark, litchen-covered, chaotic mass of broken rock forms the summit; to the north and south the ascent is gradual, but on either side it is almost perpendicular for many feet, then curves outward and is covered by the dark evergreens. We gazed down from the dizzy height,

" We heard the troubled flow
Of the dark olive depths of pines, resounding
A thousand feet below."

We marked our homeward course through the glistening lakes, away around the blue serrated summit of Mount Seward, then started on our descent. A sudden exclamation from our guide brought us to his side, where he was inspecting what we took to be the track of a naked foot.

"What is it?"

"A bar — been here since we went up — going down, probably, to the blueberry patch. We may see him if we go careful."

And carefully we went, following the track along out to the blueberry patch, and there we lost it. We waited, watched and ate berries until the shadow of the mountain like a great pyramid reached out and touched the little village; then we started.

"Maybe you'd better lead," said Baldwin, making a desperate effort to keep his feet from getting the advantage of him, while an ax, tin pail and sundry other articles jingled and thumped about on every side. "It bothers me to have folks treading on my heels." So lead we did — the result of which may be inferred from a remark he was overheard to make that night, to the effect that it beat somethin-or-other how them fellows came down that mountain, "and," said he, "when I'd get some ways behind I'd drop into a dog trot to catch up, then I'd hear that little fellow snicker and the long-legged one would cover six feet at a step."

WILMINGTON NOTCH.

# CHAPTER VI.

## "ON THE ROAD."

"John Brown's body lies a-mouldering in the grave,
And his soul goes marching on."—*Old Song.*

HE morning following our ascent of Old Whiteface, he had draped his shoulders in a mantle of mist, modestly hiding his face in the clouds, and although the sun came out toward noon and the clouds went scurrying across the sky like a routed army before the advance of an enemy, a legion still hung around his iron head, skulked in the rents and hollows of his furrowed side and crowded close under the lee of his protecting form. It was interesting to watch this vast host — this white-robed army of the sky — seeming almost human in its maneuverings to gain a place of safety from the fierce west winds which tore it into fragments and strung it out into shreds, and rolled it up into great balls to be dashed against the mountain, and separating, pass on either side to wheel into line beyond, or entering the surface current mount up the steep, and shooting out over the sharp crest, curl downward into the billowy mass below, where it clung like some tattered signal of distress, its ragged, wind-whipped end stretching away out toward the east.

After dinner we took a carriage, sandwitched the driver between us, and started for North Elba. Att. Clyne was the driver's name, a pleasant young fellow, who had rather hear or tell a good story than to eat, and that is saying a good deal for him. He inaugurated a series by telling of the wonderful speed of the particular beast behind which we were riding, the truth of which he would demonstrate when we arrived at a suitable piece of road. We never came to that suitable piece. Once we thought we had, and he encouraged her a little with the whip. She felt encouraged for about ten feet, and then rested while we got out and strapped a couple of pieces of whiffletree together which we had discovered dangling at her feet; then we went ahead carefully. About two miles south of Wilmington is the natural flume, a long furrow through the rock like the track of a giant plowshare, through which the water shoots like a flash of light. Some call it a wonder; but, with the fellow at Niagara, we might say "it would be a greater wonder if the water *didn't* come down, it comes so easy." Our road still led up along the river, now flashing out broad in the sunlight as it rippled over the stones, now quiet, and then plunging over the "big falls" seeming to lose itself in the cavernous depths below.

WILMINGTON PASS is the natural gateway to North Elba from the north, a notch cut out of the mountain, through which the west branch of the Ausable flows, it is one of the finest, if not *the* finest, combination of river, rock and mountain scenery to be found in the Adirondacks, and was especially beautiful in its autumn dress, as we saw it on that early October day. The road ran along up by the river, fringed and canopied by the crimson and yellow maples, the great, ragged, rough-armed birches, the cone-shaped balsam, the dainty-limbed tamarack and scarlet-berried mountain ash. The pass seems to have been caused by some mighty power that turning neither to the right nor left, struck this mountain range and passed through and onward, carrying every thing before it out on the plain beyond, leaving the broken walls on either side to frown down on the torn rocks below, and, when the tempest raged, to thunder back defiance at each other. Then time covered the rocks with mosses, the floods brought rich offerings and dropped them in the bottom-land, trees sprang up and others found lodgment in the cleft rocks, and now all is covered with nature's mantle. No, not *all*, for at our left, the naked rock rises up, straight up, fully five hundred feet, at places even projecting beyond its base and seeming ready to fall as great masses have already fallen, through and around which the road goes, at times with barely sufficient room to pass between them and the narrow, swift-running river on the other side. Across the river at our right is a narrow fringe of bottom-land trees, then rising, precipice above precipice, and cliff on cliff, is Old Whiteface, his feet washed by the river, his head still among the clouds, and——. There stands that fast beast out to the full extent of the reins, with the pieces of broken whiffletree on either side.

"Gr — roop!" The sound was richly musical and unmistakably African for "get-up." We were resting, if you please, three of us in a buggy, right in the middle of the road, the Professor and I rapturously enjoying the lovely scenery and innocently talking about subjects entirely foreign to the situation, while "Att." sat squeezed in between us, holding on to one end of the reins and using some very choice language in regard to the mare who stood out at the other, looking around occasionally to see why some one didn't make a move to get her back where she belonged.

"Gr-roop!" Letters cannot express the sound. The nearest approach to it is when some sea-sick mortal rushes to the vessel's side and vainly attempts to give up his own dinner to the fishes. We got out and tied the traces back to the cross-bar, put the broken whiffletree in the wagon and sent "Att." forward to make repairs.

"GR—ROOP."

"Gr-roop!" *whack!* a pair of sorry-looking objects appeared over the brow of a little knoll behind us, rising slowly as rises the stately ship above the watery horizon, first two pairs of hairy ears, then a pair of venerable heads swaying from side to side, then their entire forms loomed above the sandy horizon, and we looked up through a swaying thicket of legs and straps and wooden bars.

"Camels, by darn!" said the Professor excitedly, catching sight of what appeared to be the hump peculiar to the "ship of the desert."

No, not camels, Professor, but ancient specimens of horse architecture; style, gothic, with a tendency toward many gables, and that which you think the hump is a French roof of buffalo skin to protect them, or the harness, or both, from the rain. Framed in nature's noblest mold those beasts undoubtedly were; but the party who supplied the flesh was apparently short of material, or else they were clothed in their summer suit. Their harness fenced them in and bound them round about suggesting suspicion of a latent fire within that might, if aroused, burst forth and rend straps of an ordinary width, as the lightning shivers the mighty oak.— Straps? they crossed and covered those noble animals until they looked like a railroad map of Massachusetts, and at every crossing was a big patch of buffalo skin. They looked kindly at us, with eyes out of which all coltish frivolity had long since flown. Then the expression seemed to change to one of mild surprise as the wagon gently pressed against them and they found it easier to trot down the hill than to hold back. As they forged up alongside they stopped. They had evidently been driven by a sewing machine agent or some candidate for office, and thought they must stop for every man they saw. We instantly propounded the following conundrum to the driver:

"Why can't we ride in that extra seat?"

He gave it up at once and we got aboard the buckboard. "Gr-roop!" *whack!* we were under way. The driver was a good-looking fellow, intelligent, well-informed, and decidedly attractive in his way, even if his skin *was* a few shades darker than regulation and his hair unexplorable in its kinkiness. We inquired his destination and he told us North Elba. As St. Helena suggests the first Napoleon, so North Elba brings with it the picture of an old man with white hair and flowing white beard, crazy some said, but with wonderful method in his madness; a carpet-bagger in Kansas, where he took an active part in the troubles which in 1856 assumed the formidable proportions of a civil war; the "Old man of Osawatomie," whose presence was marked by dissensions and bloodshed; who urged men on to murder in the name of freedom and read his Bible all the time who in 1859, with a mere handful of men, struck the first hard blow at the institution of slavery in the South, and which, probably, more than the eloquence of all the Phillips and Sumners in the world, tended to precipitate the war by which, through rivers of blood, four million slaves went free. He was called "a visionary," "an old fool," but men who have given the subject study say that it was the best organized conspiracy that ever failed, reaching out as it did over the entire Southern States.

The blow struck at Harper's Ferry was to be the signal for a general uprising of the blacks, but he misjudged his men and — failed.

A fanatic he undoubtedly was. He seemed to feel that he was specially called not only to free but to educate the blacks. He secured a large tract of land here at North Elba to demonstrate his theory, and had established quite a colony. Then feeling that the time had come, he, with three sons, a son-in-law and a few others who had become converted to his belief — twenty-two in all — played at Harper's Ferry — and lost. They were soon surrounded, and the negroes, to whom they trusted so much, let them fight it out alone. One son escaped, another was shot dead, and still another lay dying by his side, while the old man fought on; and at last, when overpowered and compelled to surrender, he locked the secrets he possessed in his breast that his friends might not suffer, and died as he had lived, firm in the faith that in some manner he was the divinely appointed agent who was to lead his children out of the land of bondage. He murmured not against the people for whom he suffered, who had deserted him in his direst need, but stopped to kiss a little negro baby on his way to the scaffold, seeming to show by the act, how willingly he laid down his life for them and the cause he had espoused.

Then the body of old John Brown, the convicted murderer — this felon with the mark of the hangman's rope on his neck — was taken down from the gallows and borne through the country whose laws he had transgressed, while bells tolled and cities were draped in mourning for his sake, to his old home among the mountains — For he had said: "When I die, bury me by the big rock where I love to sit and read the word of God," and there, one terribly cold day in bleak December, a few who had loved the old man, laid his body and covered it up in the frozen ground.

"And his soul goes marching on."

Yes, the spirit of old John Brown goes marching on, and with it, keeping time to the music of the old song, whole armies marched to battle, and with the victory came that for which the old man worked and died.

"Gr-roop!" *whack!* Back to the reality of a darkey belaboring a pair of absent-minded and almost absent-bodied horses, and they supremely unconscious of the fact. We ventured to inquire if our driver was one of John Brown's pet lambs, and he with, as Mrs. Partington would say, considerable "asparagrass," gave us to understand that he was not.

"He established a colony of blacks up here, didn't he?"

"Yes, sah, but they ain't heah now. We are the only family of colo'd folks in town."

"Where are they now?"

"All gone." "Gr-roop!" *whack!* "See dat hoss — Gone; nobody knows where."

"How many were there of them?"

"Mebbe fifteen or twenty families — don't know; didn't think much of 'em."

"Slaves, I suppose, that the old man had run in here from the South?"

"No, sah, not one. G'lang!"

"Where *did* he get them?"

"Oh, from New York, mostly, I guess — not much account-Niggers. Gr-roop! what you 'bout?"

"He was generally considered a fanatic, wasn't he?"

"Sah?"

"You thought him a monomaniac?"

"A — yes, sah. Ge-*long*, thah."

"You say they are all gone; what has become of them?"

"Don't know; they couldn't make a livin' heah; too cold for 'em; wa'nt much used to work, I guess, an' couldn't stan' the kind they got heah. Most of 'em was barbers an' sich, who thought they wouldn't have nothing to do when they come heah, an' after the old man died they couldn't get along, so they dug out, some of 'em, an' some of 'em died, an' one ole niggah froze to death."

"How was that?"

"Well, he went out huntin' one day in winter and got lost in the woods. He had a compass with him, but when they found him they found where he had sat down on a log and *picked his compass to pieces*, and then sot there till he froze to death."

It is a well-known fact that some unused to the woods will become so effectually "turned around" that they will be certain that something is the matter with the compass to make it point wrong, and even distrust the sun itself if it happens to be in a different position from that which they think it *ought* to be.

"Dem hosses gettin' kinder tired," remarked their master; "don't get along over *this* road very fast."

We accepted the information with polite incredulity, as is becoming in those to whom an unnoticed fact is first made apparent.

"Been on the road a whole week —"

"Getting from the Forks?" we innocently inquired.

"Oh, no, sah; it's only fifteen miles to 'Sable Forks. I've

been carryin' a young lady 'round to see the country, drivin' them hosses steady for a week—"

"Without feeding? Well, now, I don't wonder they —"

"No, *no*, sah: I feed 'em reg'lar, only they run out all summer an' I haven't got the hard feed in 'em yet. They ain't very fat just now, but they's good hosses for all that."

Then he whipped up lively for two or three rods past a shanty, where we saw Att. busily engaged on what he was pleased to call a whiffletree, to take the place of the broken one. Then we bade good-bye to our sable friend and sat down by the river-side to make a sketch of the scene. Feeble and unsatisfactory, perhaps, but a shadow, at least a suggestion, of foaming, sparkling sun-bright water, dancing along among the stones; great, shaggy, yellow birches, golden beeches, crimson maples and tangled depths of dark green, while through openings in the trees, the gray cliff showed grand and strong, appearing even greater than itself through the tender blue of the luminous haze that intervened. Then we all got in behind the fast horse and continued on our way. Up along the river, through a dark, level tract, almost a swamp, where the balsams grew thick and the trailing moss hung in masses from their branches, out into the open country, where we saw pleasant homes, well tilled fields, and the river winding smoothly through the fertile meadows of North Elba.

After a while we came to a place where the houses were a little nearer together than anywhere else along the road, so we called that North Elba; but the population is rather thin at the best, and the country to a great extent devoted to grazing and grass growing. Winter up there seems to be the chief season and never disappoints them in coming, and it is seldom that a year passes when snow is not seen on the mountains near by every month excepting August. It is said to be very healthy, so much so that the only manner of taking off is a habit they have of freezing to death, and when this happens, as is often the case, in summer they do not find it necessary to bury them, but (if Att. is to be believed) simply lay them away somewhere exposed to the pure balsamic air and in the course of six or seven weeks they moss over. John Brown was only covered up as a protection against curiosity hunters, who have a habit of chopping off pieces of fossils and the like, and who have broken off pieces of his tombstone to such an extent that it had to be boxed up to keep enough for directory purposes.

Here at North Elba we strike the post-road, running in a north-westerly direction from Elizabethtown to the Saranac lakes. Turning to the right we proceeded about a mile until at the entrance to a lane, which led off toward the south, we saw a sign bearing the inscription, "John Brown Farm, Refreshments if desired" (at least that is what we made it out to be), together with an index finger, which was probably painted by some admirer of the old man's to indicate his present home, which direction, if followed, would take the traveler several degrees higher than we could hope to get in the Adirondacks, so we took the middle course—the lane—through a strip of woods, into the open field, and with the dusk of a solemn twilight settling down over us, stood by the great rock that he loved so well and by the side of which, at his own requst, he was buried. The farm is shut in on all sides by the thick

forests which, on the south, stretch away in unbroken solitude to Indian Pass and the great peaks of the Adirondacks. It has been purchased by a company at whose head as prime mover stands Kate Field, and now held as a sort of public park which is annually visited by hundreds who, from curiosity or reverence for the old saint, make pilgrimages to their Mecca of fanaticism. The house and outbuildings stand in the open field; near by is the "big rock" and grave, surrounded by a rough board fence.

As we entered the inclosure a little girl came out to remove the box from the headstone, which it was found necessary to cover to preserve from the destroying hand of the relic-hunter. Unlocking and removing the box we saw an old fashioned, time-stained, granite-like stone, the corners chipped and broken off, and defaced so that in places some of the inscription was entirely gone. The upper half was in the quaint characters of "ye olden time," the lower half of a recent date; the face bore the following inscription:

"In memory of Capt$^{in}$ JOHN BROW Who Died At Newyork Sept$^r$ Ye 3 1776 in the 42 year of his Age.

"JOHN BROWN Born May 9 1800 *was executed at Charleston, Va, Dec. 2. 1859.*

"OLIVER BROWN Born Mar. 9, 1839, *was Killed at Harpers Ferry* Oct. 17. 1859."

On the back was the following:

"In memory of FREDERICK son of John and Dianth Brown, Born Dec 21. 1830 and murdered at Osawatomie, Kansas, Aug 30. 1856 for his adherence to the cause of Freedom."

"WATSON BROWN, Born Oct 7, 1835 was wounded at Harpers Ferry & died Oct. 19, 1859."

The grave was strewn with faded flowers; a florist's leaden cross and crown filled with the same lay on the little mound, and under it the body of Old John Brown, alone! of his large family not one remaining to watch over him, but in their place strangers, who knew less of the old man than we who lived far away. His widow, and five children out of his twenty, are still living, it is said, scattered over the West, some of them in California, some nearer.

The stone which marks the head of his grave was brought from Massachusetts and placed where it now stands, and we were told that the "Capin" John Brown, whose name heads the list, was his father, in which case (if the Captain *was* his father) he must have been born an orphan, as this one died something over twenty-three years before young John was born. In fact there must be some mistake about it somewhere, as even after careful investigation there we could not find out that he ever *had* a father, and we would respectfully suggest that it receive the attention of the geneological authors, who, for the paltry sum of a hundred dollars, will trace any man's pedigree back in an unbroken line to dukes and earls, or better even for an additional inducement. We passed up over the big rock bearing the inscription, cut in large letters, "John Brown, 1859," and to the house to learn something more concerning it.

"Don't you want to stay all night?" said the little girl, with an eye to business.

I glanced at the grave, the cold rock and the dreary, darkening fields around, and said "No." Then a boy member of the family cornered Att., and eloquently held up to him the advantages of seeing the "stun" by daylight; but Att. couldn't see it. Then the loquacious lady of the house met the Professor at the door with the continuation of what the boy and girl had started, but the Professor being a modest man threw the responsibility on me, and, alas! all *I* wanted was information.

"We can accommodate you if you want to stay," said she, bringing the register.

We said no again, counted, and found that over four hundred besides ourselves had registered during the summer.

"Got as good rooms as anybody, and every body who has stopped here has been satisfied," continued she insinuatingly.

"Almost everybody buy these," said the little girl, producing a pair of stereographs of the grave and rock; "fifty cents for the two."

We meekly produced the plaster and inquired if they owned the place.

"No," said the mother, "we've only been here a little while, but take in strangers who want to stay all night and—"

"This is the house old John Brown used to occupy, isn't it?"

"Yes, but we've fitted it up new some since, and now you can't find any better rooms—"

"What has become of the widow and children?"

"I don't know just where, but out West somewhere, I believe. We just take care of it and keep folks who—"

"It seems to be all forests to the south; is there a path leading from here to the Indian Pass?"

"Yes, parties often come through it and stop over night or get something to eat; and I don't like to say it myself, but they always seem satisfied with our fare. Now—"

"I am gathering information for a book on the Adirondacks, which is my reason for asking so many questions. Now if you have any interesting information concerning this locality I will be—"

"Well, now, I think if people knew that we were prepared to keep folks and was always prepared to get up meals, with game and trout always on hand, they would come more; and if you will just state—"

"All right; *good* evening, madam."

"We should like to—folks say they were just as well kept as at a hotel—might just mention trout—game dinners—venison nearly all the time—barn room—people—haven't—found—it—out—much—yet—it's—getting purty—dark—hadn't—you—better—stay. And as we passed out of hearing the thought would come that if the old man could sleep there unmoved for a term of years, the angel Gabriel would have to be in pretty good lip to start him at the end of that time.

We had aimed to stay at Lake Placid on the night of our visit to the grave of John Brown, but when we reached the main road, decided to stop at the North Elba Hotel; so, boldly advancing we stirred up the old Lyon and ordered supper.

Lyon's Hotel is a very pretty little two-story house, with wings extending out from the main part, and will accommodate about 25 guests. It is situated on the post road, between Elizabethtown and Saranac Lake, 25 miles from the former—10 from the latter, and two miles from Lake Placid, with good brook fishing near by. Mr. Lyon is one of those sturdy farmer-looking men who, besides being postmaster, justice of the peace and nobody knows what all, is considered to have a sort of fatherly interest in every thing going on in the neighborhood. The literature displayed was of the most solid character: History, a Gazetteer, Congressional Proceedings, "with the compliments" of the law-makers, etc., but we felt more like devouring the supper, which was like the literary food — substantial — afterward, we disappeared for the night. See page 169.

## CHAPTER VII.

### Lake Placid.

ON the morning we started for Lake Placid. Retracing our course of the night before for a few rods we turned toward the north, and passing through a piece of woods nearly a mile in extent came out upon the shores of Mirror Lake.

MIRROR LAKE is a pretty sheet of water about one mile in length by half that in width, and was known as " Bennett's Pond " until an enthusiastic young lady composed a lot of poetical stuff concerning it and gave it its present euphonious name. (There! that word has worried me. I have been trying for some time and am thankful that I have disposed of it at last very nicely. My attention was attracted to it at first by noticing that every one who wrote about Lake George worked in "euphonious" in some way or other. I have more in reserve which I intend to precipitate on the reader at some future time.)

NASH'S, near the north end of Mirror Lake, is well known and liked by sportsmen — will accommodate about 25; J. V. Nash, the proprietor, is the oldest settler in that neighborhood; an experienced guide, although he does not practice it of late unless for particular friends, and an enthusiastic sportsman withal. (For particulars, see page 169.)

THE LAKE PLACID HOUSE, a little beyond Nash's, usually spoken of as "Brewster's," is a large comfortable looking house with broad piazza on two sides, standing on the ridge that separates Mirror Lake from Lake Placid but a few rods distant, and is deservedly a popular resort; its proprietor, Mr. Brewster, impressed me as a man who would conscientiously do all in his power for the comfort of his guests. The house is new, rooms large, comfortably furnished, and the table good.

Lake Placid is called by some the gem of the Adirondacks; but while it possesses many attractions, there are probably others equally fine. It is about five miles long and two broad, measured through the islands, of which there are three, and which are so large that the lake resembles a large river sweeping around them rather than a lake with islands.

Since leaving Wilmington we had passed south nearly half way round Whiteface Mountain, and looked to it from the south-west to where it seemed to rise directly up out of the lake, although in fact removed nearly two miles. A small pond near by attracts some attention, having the name of "Paradox Pond." It is connected with Lake Placid, by its outlet, which is also its inlet, being each in turn, and through which it is said its waters ebb and flow like the ceaseless motion of the tide.

Both Nash and Brewster have made extensive preparations for the accommodation of visitors, supplying guides, horses, boats, and every thing necessary for the use of the sportsman. They have a number of those long Adirondack boats, perfect models of beauty, and so light that a man will walk off with one on his shoulders in a way that *looks* easy enough, although a person unused to it will probably think, before he has carried it any great distance, that it is equal to a good-sized steamboat.

After dinner, we succeeded in removing Att. from the presence of a fascinating divinity in calico, and started for Saranac Lake; then as we neared that place we concluded to push on to Paul Smith's, going by way of Bloomingdale. Bloomingdale has a very pretty name, a very new looking hotel, a very few houses, a very good looking frame, which was started for a church, and now stands, considerably darkened by time, patiently waiting to be roofed and clapboarded. It was late in the afternoon when we left Bloomingdale for Paul Smith's, and a rain threatening; but Att. knew the way perfectly because he told us so, and it was only seven or eight or nine or ten miles there, so we started, and on the way, tried an old amusement — that of asking everybody we met the distance to our place of destination, almost invariably getting for reply the distance there from the home of the one questioned. Thus we continued for some time to meet persons who gave us the distance from Bloomingdale, when we had gone at least one-third the distance. It was interesting but hardly satisfactory, especially when night descended and the rain came down on our umbrella-less heads, and trickled down our necks and settled in the seat beneath us.

"Here's where we turn," said Att., wheeling around to the left. Then he pulled up to inquire the distance of a man at the side of the road.

" 'Bout six miles if you turn round and go t'other way," said the man.

Att. turned around; he knew the way, of course. Such a good joke. A little way further we found that it was four miles to Smith's; then an individual reckoned it was about seven miles, and then as we failed to meet any one else to inquire of, we had to trust in Providence and tell stories the rest of the way. The rain pattered down in a contented sort of way on the leaves and on the muddy road, and dripped from the branches of the trees and our hats and noses, and the horse got tired and wanted to walk all the way, and jokes wouldn't crack any more on account of the dampness.

We were thankful that Att. knew all about the way, but he was *so* comical and full of spirits, that he had to give every guide-post a critical examination, and the last one that we came to at the forks of the road which led out into the dark woods, he got out, and hugged and kicked and grunted up to the shingle on top, and after sacrificing sundry matches, he, with his eyes and fingers and great difficulty, succeeded in finding out that he couldn't tell any thing about it, so he slid down, and in a drizzly, uncertain sort of way, got in, and we started again. Then we recollected the line of telegraph poles that ran along by the road and were jubilant, for we knew that by following it we would bring up at Paul Smith's. So we went by telegraph the rest of the way.

"This road isn't much traveled," said Att. as we plunged down a hill into what looked like a tunnel, through overhanging trees.

"Never mind; *don't you see the telegraph?*" We were bound to stick to that as our last hope. Then the horse seemed to drop out of the harness, the wagon gave a lurch to one side and nearly lost its load, brought up and went the other way, and after jerking about like a man with two wooden legs trying to get down a pair of stairs, rested at the bottom of a gully which had been dug out by some freshet, and considered so bad that they had built a road around rather than repair it. Luckily our tired horse had taken the center and thereby kept us right side up. Att. was proud of her—"so kind and gentle," she was all of that, and more; for a persevering, go-ahead-and-ask-no-question sort of beast, I never saw her equal. If she couldn't have stood on her feet she probably would have slid down, or rolled, whichever was the easiest.

A little way further we saw a dusky strip of water through a grove of tall pines, on the shore a large house, from which lights gleamed and welcomed us onward, and we were soon seated around a crackling fire, with a room full of guides, dogs and sportsmen, who smoked and told stories until the clock struck twelve, and we went to sleep listening to the patter of the raindrops on the roof.

"PAUL SMITH'S."

"PAUL SMITH'S" is a suprise to everbody; an astonishing mixture of fish and fashion, pianos and puppies, Brussels carpeting and cowhide boots. Surrounded by a dense forest; out of the way of all travel save that which is its own; near the best hunting and fishing grounds (for the matter of that,

## ST. REGIS LAKE.

however, they are *all* the very best, if the veracious guide books are to be relied on); a first-class watering-place hotel, with all the modern appliances, and a table that is seldom equaled in the best of city hotels, set right down in the midst of a "howling wilderness." Around the house the timid deer roam; within, they rest. Without, the noble buck crashes through the tangled forest; within, his noble namesake straddles elegantly over the billiard tables and talks horse. Out on the lake the theoretical veteran casts all manner of flies; in the parlors the contents of huge Saratoga trunks are scientifically played, and nets are spread for a different kind of fish. Poodles and pointers, hounds, setters, dandies and others of the species are found. Feathers and fishing rods, point lace and pint bottles, embryo Nimrods — who never knew a more destructive weapon than a yard-stick — hung all around with revolvers and game-bags and cartridge-pouches and sporting guns that are fearfully and wonderfully made, and which would take a first-class engineer to work; for you must know that here danger is to be faced, that even the ladies bare arms, and are said at such times to be very dangerous sportsmen indeed.

The St. Regis lake consists of two, the upper and lower. The upper lake is about five miles long, the water passing through "Spitfire Pond" to the lower lake, and out through the St. Regis river to the St. Lawrence. The lower lake is about two miles long and one in width, being nearly 2,000 feet above tide, on that great level plateau north and west of the "great peaks." The surrounding country is rather tame, lacking the high mountains which are found further south.

PAUL SMITH came here in 1861, built a small house among the pines, and commenced keeping sportsmen, in which he was very successful, and at present shows a large, three-story hotel, with ample accommodations for over one hundred guests, besides a large house for the use of guides, and a fine set of stables for his own and other horses that may come. It is thirty-seven miles to "Point of Rocks," the southern terminus of the Plattsburgh railroad, to which place, during the season, a daily line of stages are run. The telegraph, which is carried into the house, places its occupants within talking distance of the outer world, and speaks well for the enterprise of the proprietor.

In appearance he is not the man you would pick out as the one to keep a popular hotel. Rather above medium height, usually quiet, not appearing to have much to say about the house nor much to do but listen to stories and perform other like laborious duties usually expected of the keeper of a summer hotel. But *somebody* there must possess executive ability, for all seems to go as smoothly as clock-work, and, gazing at the quiet Paul the words of the poet came dreamily to me, where he says something about "the still sow getting most of the swill."

The fond parents of the gentleman alluded to, when he was a youngster, broke away from the established custom of the rather extensive family to which they belonged, and utterly refused to name their offspring " John ; " calling him instead, "Apolus A. Smith." *Apolus* is a Scripture name — " Paul may plant and *Apolus* water," etc. Whatever curious bearing the name may have had in the matter is unknown ; but he planted himself where the water would be handy if he should ever need it, and from Apolus his name was soon bobbed down to "Pol," then to " Paul " by those who were disgusted to find that ' Pol " was only a man ; and now, a letter directed to "Apolus A. Smith " would be very liable to be sent to the Dead Letter Office by the owner of the name himself. At all events, Paul Smith's is a very popular resort, and patronized extensively by a wealthy class of visitors, who prefer to rough it in a voluptuous sort of way.

Although rather late in the season when we were there, a few kindred spirits still lingered, who were personally and intimately acquainted with everybody, from the Shah and Yankee Sullivan down to the Heathen Chinee, and who, when night came, would gather around the stove in the office, and to an appreciative audience of dogs, guides and themselves, would review the drama, the arts and sciences, tell stories of fighting men and ministers, dogs and horses, hunting and fishing, interspersed with intensely interesting debates on the relative merits of plug and fine-cut, and give learned disquisitions on the proper position of the left auricle at that exciting moment when the fly has been cast, and a gamey two ounce trout has struck, and hesitates as to the expediency of taking to the woods or the open field. On this much vexed question authorities differ, and it is probable that it will always be a disputed point, as the physical development and temperament of the fish has to be taken into consideration. A fisherman as is a fisherman must be governed by circumstances — quick to take advantage of mistakes. In fact he must be a strategist of superior calibre, even like unto that of the most successful fisherman of whom we have any record, who, after the fashion in those primitive days before they used "flies" as extensively as at present, swallowed a whale, and after a three days' struggle succeeded in bringing him safely to land.

Sunday morning it rained. On account of the day the stories had a subdued sort of spirit in them, and the principal business was to get through with three meals and go to bed. Monday morning it rained. Got up, dressed, ate breakfast and listened to stories; ate dinner, heard some stories; had supper, after which there were some stories told, interspersed here and there with stories, and occasionally a story to give zest to the entertainment which consisted principally of stories. Then more stories, and after another story or two we went to bed with a confused sort of an idea that a swarm of green and red and white and black and brown and yellow and "scarlet ibes" and "green dragon flies," with lines tied to their heads and fish-hooks in their tails, sported playfully around our heads, floated enticingly near us, was scientifically cast or tantalizingly skittered across the water, tempting us to "rise;" but our eyes were opened to the miserable cheats of the anglers who were not repaid by a single "strike," while we floated out into deep water and thus ended our last day at Paul Smith's.

We had engaged a guide to go with us from Paul Smith's through the Saranacs to Long Lake, but when we opened our eyes on the morning of the 7th of October the ground was white with snow, and the trip had to be given up.

"By darn!" said the Professor, with an air of desperation, "I don't want to be snowed in up here in the woods all winter; doesn't a stage leave here for somewhere?"

We found that one would go anywhere for a consideration, so we engaged it to take us to Martin's at the north end of the lower Saranac, distant about fourteen miles by road and thirty by water—the route we had intended to take if the weather had been suitable.

How indescribably lovely the landscape appeared that morning. The great flakes danced and whirled and floated, crossing back and forth as if in play with each other as they fluttered downward through the air, covering every stone and tree and shrub, clinging to the delicate tamarac and hemlock, weighing down the sturdy spruce and pines until their branches bowed gracefully beneath the load, changing the climbing vines into a delicate tracery of white, the long, wavy grasses and graceful ferns into frosted silver and the surrounding woods into a grand, pure forest of pearl and milk-white glass; and when we reached the open country new beauties came into sight; the fields, stretching away in their dress of white, through which stone and stubble could be seen, softening and subduing the foreground, while fainter far away the hills rose up until lost in the falling clouds of beautiful snow. Soon we became conscious that we had left the main road and were on one which required some little attention on our part to keep from doing injury to the interior of the stage. It was a good road—for a dyspeptic or one troubled with a poor appetite; the ride cost us six dollars, but we got our money's worth—there was so much variety to it, the driver was apparently in something of a hurry; it was a good stage, too, and we being the only occupants we had a choice of position. We tried several; braced ourselves up in the corners; we rattled all around lively like; we shot from side to side; made some good runs, caromed on each other and pocketed ourselves under the seats. We couldn't get knocked out, for the sides —excepting a look-out hole—were buttoned down and the roof was firm—we were satisfied of that, for we tried it. Sometimes the Professor's side would rise up to get over a big stone and he would start for me. I had repeatedly striven with him and remonstrated against such frequent and energetic calls and unceremonious visitations, but to no effect, retribution was sure to follow however, when his side went down, for then I would sail majestically over and light on him. Sometimes that vehicle would meander playfully over stones and stumps and into holes, shucking us all about; then it would jump up over a log and we, rising like young eagles, would soar away toward the roof. We liked to soar, but couldn't light worth a cent. Then it would go down into deep holes and stop in such a decided sort of way that we would involuntarily feel our heads, expecting to find our backbones sticking up through our hats; and when at last we reached Saranac Lake it was with a feeling of "goneness" peculiar to those who have been without food for — say nine or ten months, or a year for instance.

"MARTIN'S."

"MARTIN'S" is about the same distance from Point-of-Rocks as "Paul Smith's," viz.: 37 miles, and is at the regular gateway to the Saranac and Tupper's Lake regions. Wm. F. Martin, its proprietor, came here in 1849 and built a small house for the accommodation of sportsmen, he being among the very first to attempt a sporting house in the wilderness. He is a thorough woodsman and hunter, and that he knows how to keep a hotel is demonstrated by the large business worked up at his place. The house is on the shore of the lake at its northern extremity; will accommodate 200; is well furnished throughout, and is very popular, although not quite as fashionable as "Paul Smith's," in the high-toned sense of the word.

SARANAC LAKE FROM MARTIN'S.

## CHAPTER VIII.

### THE LOWER SARANAC.

THE morning after our arrival, we started for the upper lake in one of Bartlett's freight boats which chanced to be going up at that time. It was a lovely morning — a little frosty to be sure, but not uncomfortable — and the sun came out soon, clear and warm, raising delicate wisps of mist from the surface of the water and making the snow-laden trees glitter with their millions of diamonds, and the naked summits of the high mountains — Whiteface on the north-east and Marcy, with its surrounding peaks, away to the south-east — reflected in the glassy lake like great mountains of shining snow. The lower lake is six miles long, and said to contain 52 islands, one for each week of the year; the shores, picturesque; at times rising in solid rock straight up, at others, shelving smoothly out into the deep water.

At the south-west end of the lake, "in the shadow of a great rock," we entered a river fringed with flags and lily-pads and tall, dead trees, marking what was once the shores, now covered with water — the effect of a dam which was built at the outlet of the lake, adding four feet to its original level and flooding back up this stream for something over a mile. A great many of the lakes and ponds of the wilderness have been dammed by the lumbermen and held in reserve for times when the volume of water in the beds of the rivers is not sufficient to carry the logs along, when the gates are hoisted and the flood goes down carrying every thing before it. The result of this overflow of the natural boundaries of the lakes has been to kill the vegetation on the shores, and the beauty of many of them has been seriously impaired by this border of dead and dying trees. Something over a mile was passed when we came to the falls — but little more than rapids — where the water shoots down through a smooth, rocky channel, with a *swish* and a curl or two at the bottom. We stepped ashore, and while one held the boat away from the rock the rest pulled it up through the cut, then got aboard and picked our way slowly up stream.

The ordinary Adirondack boat is a model of beauty, long and narrow, nearly alike at the ends, although above the water-line it is widened out somewhat, seldom enough, however, to allow a small boy to sit away back in the stern, all of which is well enough in a small boat, but the principle seems grotesque enough when applied to one that will carry a ton. Our craft was of the stereotyped mould and dragged heavily, at times requiring the help of all to push and paddle her over the bars. We suggested that a part of the cargo be carried further forward to trim ship properly, but the captain — there was a captain and one crew — allowed that he had loaded a good many boats in his life and never had to shift the load either (actual measurement showed that we drew 2 inches of water forward and 18 at the stern), still his position was triumphantly maintained until we dragged over the sandy bottom into

Round Lake and up to Bartlett's followed by a series of swells such as follow in the wake of a propeller.

Round Lake is about two and one-half miles in diameter and, as its name implies, nearly round in shape. It contains several very pretty rocky islands, and although the surrounding country is quite level, the shores are bold and at that time were brilliant in their autumn dress. Passing across we went out on the west side between two great rocks, and up a slow stream half a mile, to the hotel.

BARTLETT'S.

Bartlett's is at the foot of the short carry, between Round Lake and the upper Saranac. Here the boats are taken from the water and transported to the upper lake on a cart at a cost of fifty cents for each boat. The house, which will accommodate about fifty, is a long, low, old-fashioned structure, with a rambling, uncertain look about it and its out-buildings, as though they were dropped down here and there as a temporary sort of arrangement. The interior is pleasant, containing some fine and well-furnished rooms; the table is excellent. It is reached principally by the route we pursued and has no connection with the outer world save by boat or through the wild woods. The proprietor, Mr. Bartlett, has lived there for many years, and his host of friends will regret to learn that he is to give up the business.

"Yes," said he, "I've had enough of it. I've slaved as long as I am going to, and I'm going to sell out. Never'll take another boarder as long as I live, unless it be some old friend, like Dr. Ely, for instance." He did not say who would occupy his old stand, but whoever it may be it will require considerable talent to fill the old proprietor's place, for he is well liked, as is also Mrs. Bartlett, who impressed me as being a lady of refinement and culture. Mr. Bartlett is a short, thick-set man, with a brusque way of speaking that sounds cross until you catch the kindly twinkle in his eye. My numerous questions concerning his affairs seemed to bother him until I explained that, in a small way, I was connected with the press.

"The press!" said he, with a snap; "darn the press! I've been pressed to death. I don't want any thing more to do with it; I don't care what they say about me." Then, with that twinkle in his eye, he told of some things that the press had said of him, which showed him to be not entirely lost to its blandishments.

All, or nearly all, of the sporting houses advertise to furnish fishing-tackle and everything required for the sport; so after dinner we decided to take a trip through the upper lake and return at night (as the course we had marked out simply led across the south end of it), and thought it would do no harm to put out a trolling-line — possibly we might strike something — so we applied to the clerk for the necessary articles. He didn't appear particularly anxious to spring around and produce them. He was devoted to his duties which called for his presence behind a little desk that fenced off one corner of the room, and afforded a safe retreat for himself and sundry mysterious-looking bottles. Some folks would have taken it for a bar; but, bless you! it was no such thing. At least the only things called for were "opodeldoc" and "laughing-gas," and everybody knows that neither of those articles are spirituous. At last he said he would try to rig me up, so he started. In the course of a half-hour I found him sitting contentedly on the porch, where he had stopped to rest, and was soothed with the information that he didn't believe there was any use of trying to troll. I thought so myself, but nevertheless wanted to do it as long as I had set out with that intention, so he started again. After another lapse of valuable time I set out once more and found him in the guide-house, serenely seated on a dry goods box, swinging his legs back and forth and drumming with his fingers in a dreary sort of way. I was anxious and had to interrupt his reverie. I said:

"Where's that line?"

"Hain't got none;" then he whistled a little tune.

"But don't you advertise to supply such things?"

The question didn't seem to interest him much, but he stopped whistling long enough to say, "Yes."

"Well, can you do it?"

My perseverance in the insane desire seemed to excite a mild surprise in his brain and he said that Bartlett had had some that summer, but he guessed they were all lost; anyway he didn't know where they were. I was told that if the proprietor had been at home I would have had no trouble, as he was always ready to help his guests in every way possible. But I don't blame the clerk, not a bit, he was overworked; nearly tired out at the time and did give out entirely so that he had to be put to bed quite early that evening. At last, by aid of our guide, we succeeded in getting a line, and started.

The Upper Saranac is about eight miles long and perhaps two wide, the longest way being north and south. It discharges toward the east from its south end through an arm which is nearly two miles deep, then making quite a rapid descent for the distance of a hundred rods to where, at its foot, is situated Bartlett's — our stopping-place. It contains a number of rocky islands, some of them high and bold. The shores are thickly wooded and picturesque, the country around quite level, and the hills about can scarcely lay claim to the title of mountain. At its head — the terminus of the road to Bloomingdale, fourteen miles distant — is the Prospect House, a clean, white building with a thrifty look about it that speaks volumes in its favor.

We reached Bartlett's soon after dark, and I didn't get a

bite, although I fished faithfully. Perhaps the velocity of our boat had something to do with our ill-luck; as the "gang" to which a shiner was attached would spring out of the water occasionally, and "skitter" along the surface like any thing but a fish; but the spirit of Isaac Walton moved within me, and I felt the excitement of the veteran angler at the very sound of the word "fish." I had admired Murray for his wonderful skill, devoured the contents of "I go-a-fishing" with avidity and felt able to play any thing and throw any kind of a fly in existence. In imagination, with the great piscatorial lights of the age, I had felt my heart thrill at sight of a polywog and closed my eyes in an ecstacy of bliss, as I thought of the terrific ravings of a half-ounce sucker when fairly *fast*. With such feelings surging through my breast we went in to supper. Ah! can it be possible? Yes, *yes*. it is! it is!! A school of fish-balls within easy reach! I will catch one; but what true fisherman can act the part of a butcher? True greatness in that line consists not in the amount bagged, but the manner of doing it. My heart thrilled with the excitement which the angler feels when the gently undulating motion of the atmosphere tells him that his game is nigh. I prepared for a cast. A moment's hesitation, in which the momentous question presented itself whether I had better take my "scarlet dragon" or "blue-tailed ibes." I tried both, but not a ripple stirred the quiet depths; then I tried a spoon. Now I contend that it requires a great deal of skill to cast a spoon properly for a fish-ball, especially at this season of the year. Carefully I played it around over the bread; dragged it slowly across the potatoes, skittered it lightly over the butter and let it drop where I knew the wary creatures were lying in wait. Slowly it settled down, lightly as the dew into the heart of a blushing rose. A gentle ripple stirred the surface; I felt intuitively that the trying moment had come. A thrill shot up my arm and throughout my body to the very pit of my stomach as the beautiful creature curled upward and struck — struck hard. Then began the struggle for life on the one side against science on the other — mind against matter. It is an undoubted fact that an intellectual man, with a good spoon, is more than a match for any fish-ball in existence. Carefully I played him, for it was a gamey fish-ball. The surrounding gravy was lashed into fury and foamed white as the driven snow, but the cruel spoon held him, and with a sullen shaking he rested on the bottom — preparing for another run. Now he darts away like a flash of light, and is brought up by my gradually, though firmly compressing arm; then he turned, and as he passed he clove his native element as the thunder-bolt might cleave a summer squash; but the spoon brought him up once more and he turned directly toward us. It was a critical moment — a moment of terrible suspense.

"Give him the butt!" screamed the Professor, dodging behind the teapot; "give him the butt!"

"Stand firm, Professor!" I cried, wrought up to the highest pitch of excitement as the enraged fish-ball sprang seventeen feet in the air and made directly for me with my mouth wide open; "stand firm, and the victory is ours."

I gave him the butt as he came, and the delicate rod bent as a reed shaken in the wind. Oh! the terrific fire that blazed from the eye of that fish-ball will haunt me till my dying day. Rage, agony, despair, all blended in one as, shaking the sparkling drops of water from his gleaming sides he sprang entirely over us — plunged downward on the other side and again renewed the attack. But I desist. Suffice it to say that at the expiration of an exciting hour and fifty-nine minutes sport, I succeeded in safely landing that heroic creature and laid him, a conquered fish-ball, at my feet. Science had triumphed.

Mr. Murray says, that "the highest bodily beatitude he ever expects to reach, is to sit in a boat with John at the paddle, and match again a Conroy rod against a three-pound trout;" but as for *me*, give me my trusty spoon, or even a sharp stick. I care not *who* sits at the paddle, and let *me* once more feel the deathless joy of a single handed encounter with an untamed fish-ball, and I'll murmur not even though a yawning legislature opens and sucks me in forever. Pardon this ebullition, but I can never keep cool when so terribly excited, and right here, let me lift my voice against the horrible practice of some coarse natures whose soul never swept upward to a spiritual conception of flies, and who, with no excuse, save perhaps that of hunger, can, with a common hook and line, and filthy worms for bait, snatch a kingly trout baldheaded, and lay him gasping in uncomfortable terror on the ground. We cannot find words of condemnation strong enough to express our horror of this barbarous practice, which is extremely vulgar, contributes nothing to science, and is in all probability excessively annoying to the fish.

On the contrary, the scientific allurement of a denizen of the aqueous fluid to one more volatile is an achievement worthy of a great intellect. The skillful playing prepares the noble creature for its final transition which, if not actually attended with pleasurable sensations to the subject in question, must be owing to its lack of appreciation of the important part it is playing in the march of intellect. It is also more christian-like and refined than bull baiting, because less dangerous, and we cannot wonder that great minds — divines even — are sometimes translated by its wonderful fascinations.

### TUPPER LAKE REGION.

At Bartlett's, three great wilderness routes diverge, one toward the north through the Upper Saranac and other lakes to Paul Smith's on the St. Regis, another west to the Tupper lake region, and a third, south to Long and Raquette lakes.

About two miles west of Bartlett's is the old Sweeny Carry, now operated by the Daniels' Brothers, who live at its east and west ends, three miles apart, transporting boats and luggage across at $1.50 per load when required. The western terminus rests on Raquette river which, followed down eleven miles, touches Big Tupper's lake at its outlet. Here at the foot — a little to the left — is a very comfortable wildwood hotel kept by Martin Moody, with accommodations for fifty guests. Moody is an old hunter and guide, and is perfectly familiar with the lake region for miles around, which, together with the location, renders his place very desirable to the sportsman. (See page 170.)

The country is comparatively level, while it has, in reality, a mountain air, being a part of that vast elevated plateau which goes to make up so much of the western portion of the wilderness, and although Mt. Morris may fairly be called a mountain, standing where it does, it would hardly be noticed among the great peaks.

TUPPER'S LAKE is six miles in extent, contains a number of picturesque islands, some rocky and barren, others covered with verdure; the shores are bold, at one place rising to a height of seventy feet. A rocky bluff well worth inspection, is known as the Devil's Pulpit, although why, or what he could possibly want of such an article will probably remain a mystery for some time to come. Another object of peculiar beauty and interest is the water of Bog river, hanging like a ribbon of silver down over the face of the cliff at the head of the lake. Besides Moody's, there are three other families near the foot, namely, Stetson, McLaughlin and McBride, making, for that region, what is considered a large settlement, and although somewhat crowded, they seem to live harmoniously enough, compressed, as they are, within the circuit of a mile or two. Near the head of the lake is "Graves' Lodge," another sporting house of some note. From Graves' a route leads over a three mile carry to Horseshoe pond, then by boat with an occasional carry, through chain ponds, twelve miles further to that dismal sheet of waters known as Mud lake.

MUD LAKE is less than two miles in extent the longest way, covered in their season with lily-pads and margined with rank wild grass, a favorite feeding spot for deer, if not indeed the best in the entire wilderness, and also noted as a breeding place for those Adirondack luxuries — black flies and mosquitoes, which, together with its lonely position, serves to keep sportsmen from becoming too familiar with its waters. Around this dark lake and away from its head stretches a natural meadow where of old the moose came to feed in vast numbers, before their ranks were thinned by the hunters, then one by one they fell, until at last it was thought not one remained in the wilderness, the last of his race being shot, it is said, about fifteen years ago by Governor Seymour in the John Brown tract. Of late, however, signs have been seen at Mud lake, and last summer, it is claimed, the fresh tracks of a three-year old moose were found in Herkimer county by Charles Fenton who is authority for the statement, and not supposed to be easily mistaken, as he has hunted these animals repeatedly. Let us hope that it is indeed so and that when the wilderness shall be created a great public park, the protecting arm of the law will be thrown around its denizens, and once more the ground may tremble beneath the tread of the mighty moose.

CRANBERRY LAKE is seven miles north of Mud lake, one of the largest of the Adirondack series, being about fifteen miles in length, discharges through the Oswegatchie river toward the north, and is usually visited from the west via Gouverneur. Another route from Tupper's lake leads south through Round pond to Little Tupper's, thence through a chain of ponds to Long lake; still another from the head of Little Tupper's passes through Charley pond, Smith's and Albany lakes; then through pond and brook to Oswegatchie river, and north into Cranberry lake; in short, there is no end to the routes, and if the tourist is not satisfied with the amusement at the end of the last one named, he must be an enthusiastic sportsman indeed.

THE INDIAN CARRY, at the southern extremity of the Upper Saranac, is nearly two miles from Bartlett's. Located here is an old settler, who, like nearly all the inhabitants of the great wilderness, keeps a hotel, which is half frame, half log, with accommodations for about a dozen guests. As we approached, a young man who had anticipated our wants, appeared on the shore with a horse attached to a wagon, on which we easily lifted our light boat, that, with scarcely a moment's delay, was going over land to Stony creek.

This is the noted Indian carry, a smooth road running through a belt of cleared land, one mile in length; at the southern end is another family, who, with Corey at the north, haul boats and baggage over at seventy-five cents per load. It is said that years ago an Indian village stood here on what was one of their principal highways — hence the name.

THE SPECTACLE PONDS, or Stony creek ponds, are three in number; the first a few rods in extent, the second — into which we went through a reedy gate — about a mile the longest way; the third very like the first. As we passed out the deep baying of a hound attracted our attention, and almost at the same moment a noble buck came down the hillside on the east, stood motionless, until our guide, who was young to the woods and appeared suddenly attacked with the buck fever, fired four times at him, then turned and bounded away, touching the ground daintily as a butterfly, or as a feather blown along by the wind, with that peculiar undulating motion so wonderful in an animal weighing, as he did, two hundred pounds at the least.

"I'm glad of it," said the Professor, and so was I, although for the moment the soul of a Nimrod had struggled within me and I longed to "draw a bead" on him.

STONY CREEK, applied to the stream which we entered, is a misnomer. It runs about three miles in making what in a straight line is but little more than *one*; slow, sluggish, running through a swamp, its shores lined with tall grass and the sprawling, ragged swamp-maples that seem to flourish best in a watery soil. We met two or three parties, apparently bound homeward, and then came out and floated on the red waters of the Raquette. From the mouth of Stony Creek down the Raquette it is twenty miles to Big Tupper lake.

Mother Johnson's is on the Raquette, seven miles above  Stony Creek. All admirers of the Rev. W. H. H. Murray, and readers of his romantic and perilous adventures in the Adirondacks, will remember his struggle with the pancakes, and Mother Johnson is the one who had the honor of providing them. We reached the house at noon, and the good-natured old lady got up a splendid dinner for us; venison that had (contrary to the usual dish set before us) a juiciness and actual taste to it. Then she had a fine fish on the table.

"What kind of a fish is that, Mrs. Johnson?" I inquired.

"Well," said she, "they don't have no name after the 15th of September. They are a good deal like trout, but it's against the law to catch trout after the fifteenth, you know."

MOTHER JOHNSON.

Mother Johnson moved here with her husband in 1870, and they pick up a good many dollars during the season from travelers, who seldom pass without getting at least one meal. Boats are dragged over the carry nearly two miles in extent, and a very rough road at that, on an ox sled, at a cost of $1.50. A few rods above the house is Raquette Falls, laying claim to the honor of being Mr. Murray's "Phantom Falls." The actual fall here is probably not over twelve or fifteen feet. Mother Johnson entertains a very exalted opinion of Mr. Murray, with good reason, too, as his Adirondack book first turned the tide of travel past her door, and was the means of converting her pancakes (we had some) into greenbacks; and although she may subscribe heartily to the belief that "man was created a little lower than the angels," it is no more than natural that she should make an exception in the case of the Nimrodish divine alluded to.

UP THE RAQUETTE.

After dinner we followed the boat over the carry in its awful slushy, snowy muddiness, and putting it in above the rapids set out up the river once more. Here the water, that at a depth of two feet is a rich brown or red, appeared almost inky in its blackness. Sluggish in its motion, it seemed to fill the space left and fairly round up in the center. Great dark green cedars line its banks, their branches reaching out toward the light and downward thirstily toward the water, seeming in this to display their love for light and moisture, for the sides away from the river were naked and limbless. Here the river is four or five rods in width, and so still that when we passed up it seemed more like a river of black glass than water. It has slowly worn away the banks and undermined the cedars that line it until they have fallen over and stand at every conceivable angle with the surface of the stream, and as they have gradually fallen, the body, with its love for the zenith, has curled upward, the smaller limbs that at first reached down toward the water, seemingly alarmed at their too near approach, turn upward and hang in great hooks and solid festoons from their leaning supports, the whole duplicated in the mirror below, seemingly made our journey lie through grand isles of gothic arches on either side, while we floated on a thin something that held us suspended midway between the heavens above and the heavens below.

About five miles from Mother Johnson's we passed the mouth of Cold River coming down from Mount Seward on the east and supplying, by considerable, the largest volume of water of the two rivers which here meet. Above this we occasionally ran on a bar and had to pick our way carefully up. We had left the cedars, passed through the maples, now stripped of their foliage, and came out on a natural meadow, where the coarse hay had been cut and piled up on platforms resting on piles, there to stay until the ice should render them accessible to sleighs.

Over the shallow outlet we went through the tall grass, where several mounds of sticks and reeds showed the presence of a colony of muskrats, out into Long Lake and across to the Island House, where a jolly party of *spiritual* fellows were having a loud time. It is owned by John Davis at Newcomb, proprietor of the Halfway House there, and will accommodate about 30; is reached by way of Kellogg's or over the new water route opened up to Newcomb 12 miles distant, passing through Catlin and other lakes, it is 9 miles from Kellogg's and 6 from Mother Johnson's.

LONG LAKE is nearly 14 miles in length and about one mile

in width at the widest part, which is near its outlet. It runs in a north-easterly direction, receives the waters of the Raquette River at its head and gives them up to the same name at its foot. Thence, the water flowing northward, joins Cold River, and passing within about three miles of the Saranac lakes, turns toward the south-west, touching the foot of Big Tupper's Lake, then north-westerly past Potsdam to the St. Lawrence. Long Lake contains several islands; one, nearly midway between the inlet and the outlet is called Round Island, and resembles Dome Island of Lake George, only that it is more perfect in its dome-like appearance. Near the head of the lake, on the west, is the Owl's Head, a mountain marked on the map as being 2,706 feet above tide, but as Long Lake is over 1,500 above the ocean, the Owl's Head isn't much of a mountain after all. To the west the country is level; on the east is Mount Kempshall, originally called Long Lake Mountain; on the north the blue serrated summit of Mount Seward, 5,100 feet above tide.

Three or four years ago some one put a few pickerel into Long Lake to see if they would breed. The experiment was a success. They multiplied and replenished the pickerel world in a way truly wonderful; and now it is rare sport for *fishermen*, but the guides, who have been spoiled on trout and salmon, want to just get hold of the man who put the first lot in. They do not fancy the slime that goes with the fish which they call a hog, ready to bite any thing that comes along, from a dish-rag to a small boy, "plays" like a log, their "gameness" consisting of a habit they have of allowing themselves to be dragged anywhere after they are once fairly hooked.

LONG LAKE VILLAGE, commonly called "Gougeville," is situated on the east side of the lake, 3½ miles from its head. It is composed of 18 to 20 buildings, assorted sizes, a schoolhouse, church, store, post-office, and what is of more interest to the average traveler, Kellogg's popular hotel. At present, I have no vivid recollection of a "Sabbath in the woods," but in this connection do remember one spent at Gougeville three or four years ago, which was ushered in by a general brightening up of guns and sorting of fishing-tackle that indicated any thing but a devotional spirit as the word is generally understood, and seemed to show that there was a variety of opinion as to the proper manner of celebrating the day in question.

We concluded to attend divine worship and in due time found ourselves seated in the little church listening to an earnest discourse from the minister who was also blacksmith, lawyer, shoemaker and merchant in a small way, besides devoting his leisure hours to meditation and farming.

The interior was not what could properly be styled luxurious, but it was substantial. Over the pulpit, and occupying a considerable portion of that end of the building, was an immense marine clock, great in the display of gold, while letters on its face explained that it was " presented by Dr. Todd's Mission S. School," from somewhere or other — I don't remember where just now, but understand that the philanthropic donors are at present engaged in a laudable endeavor to furnish overcoats to the suffering Hottentot; it *did* seem like discouraging work for a frail mortal of a minister man to attempt to lead minds away on the ocean of eternity with time staring them so squarely in the face. Uneducated as we were in the science of mellifluous strains, we could but notice the vast difference between the rendition of familiar pieces by the choir, and the high spiced olio of sacred song dispensed by the $20,000 kind. *There* was no sinful mixing of Old Hundred with the latest operas; no voluptuous waltzes trickling down through tortured coronation; no basso profundo howlings in *Le Diable* — revamped for Sunday ears; no fancy runs, artistic slides, or coltish whinnying in the upper register, but primitive purity undefiled ruled the hour, the leader leading off gallantly, and as soon as it became known what tune he had started a female voice dashed in a half note behind making great exertions to close the gap between them. Now voice after voice took up the strain that rose and swelled until it seemed that three or four voices were blended together like a half dozen; some wandered away and foundered; the high soprana made several gallant starts ahead to pass the leader, but he kept to his knitting, and came out first — winning the heat by a good half-length, while the bass

" Came rumbling after."

Here, at Long Lake, the road from Pottersville and Schroon touches, thence turning south, continues along the east shore and south-west, past Raquette Lake, at places being little more than a mere trail and known as the Carthage road. The land around, while apparently promising well, is cold and illy adapted to farming purposes, some of the clearings having been made upwards of forty years, and quite good buildings put up, but a blight seems to have come over them, which is especially noticeable on the road toward Newcomb; the township contains about 300 inhabitants, who subsist principally by guiding through the summer, and hunting and trapping in the winter. There are several places of entertainment besides the regular hotel among them. PALMER'S, a favorite stopping place of A. F. Tait, the artist, 2½ miles south of Kellogg's, is well spoken of.

MITCHEL SABATTIS, who also keeps boarders, is a noted Indian guide, who has figured extensively in all histories of that region and deserves more than a passing notice. He was born at Parishville, St. Lawrence county, September 29, 1823, a pure blood of the tribe of St. Francis, he early took to the woods as naturally as a duck to water. On the death of his mother, which occurred when he was but seven years of age, his father, "Captain Peter," as he was universally called, used to take him along on his various hunting and

MITCHEL SABATTIS.

trapping expeditions. The Captain, who earned his right to the title by his services in that capacity during the war of the Revolution, is said to have been a noble specimen of a man — mentally as well as physically, and died in 1859 at the advanced age of 108. As a proof of his physical powers a place is still pointed out a little below Raquette Pond, known as "Captain Peter's rock," from which he once leaped to the shore, fully sixteen feet distant. Mitchel is earnest, intelligent and thrifty, a member of the Methodist church, is authority for many things relating to Indian history, has probably seen more of wood life than any other man in the wilderness, a fearless and successful hunter and is generously admitted by other guides to have the best knowledge of the woods of any man in the country. He killed his first deer when 13 years of age, and since then the number that has fallen before his unerring rifle is legion; he has also taken several bears, nine panthers — actually driving one, a huge fellow, along a narrow shelf on the face of a ledge into a crevice, from which he was dislodged by two or three vigorous punches with a sharp stick in order that a companion might get a shot at him, but for some unaccountable reason he failed to do it, and Sabattis dispatched the beast himself; on measuring, the panther was found to be 9 feet from tip to tip. In his earlier days, moose were plenty in the woods and he has killed twenty of these huge animals, the last being in 1854. The old hunter is still hale and hearty, bidding fair, with his iron constitution, to guide for many a year to come.

Long Lake has one industry wherein it stands at the head, that of boat-building, a "Long Lake boat" in the Adirondacks being considered the synonym of all that is graceful and perfect in that line, the regulation boat is about 3 feet wide, from 14 to 17 long, weighing when new, from 60 to 80 pounds, and costing about one dollar per pound.

THE LONG LAKE HOTEL, kept by C. H. Kellogg, is situated about one-fourth mile from the lake shore, a large white building, comfortably furnished, setting a good table and with a capacity for taking care of thirty guests very comfortably; a dashing little brook foams and tumbles past close by, said to yield hosts of speckled beauties, and a fleet of boats on the lake shore is at the service of those who will troll for the heavier pickerel and "lakers." Kellogg's hotel and store is a base of supplies for the region round about, and is a starting point for routes which radiate in various directions. Stages carrying the mail arrive and depart twice weekly through the sporting season, passing through Newcomb to Minerva, thence to the Adirondack railroad at North Creek, or to Pottersville at the foot of Schroon Lake, each about 41 miles distant. It is the head-quarters of a long list of guides who stand at the very head of the profession.

# CHAPTER IX.

### The Schoolmaster.

WE SENT our Saranac guide back, and inquired for one who understood the Raquette Lake region.

"I know the man you want," said our host, in a way as though he felt himself responsible for our future happiness; "Charley Blanchard knows all about it, just came from that region day before yesterday. I'll send for him."

He did so, and soon a little fellow in a Garabaldian shirt stood before us. Thinking of the work a guide is expected to do, it seemed as though this one was meant for a joke or an ornamental head that we would have to carry over the rough places. Kellogg must have noticed the look of surprise on our faces, for, taking me aside, he said:

"Oh, he's all right; knows the country better'n I do my house, and will take you right every time."

"Carry a boat too?" I asked, incredulously gazing at the slight figure.

"Yes, *sir!* carried a boat, oars and all, over the same route a day or two ago. Then he can learn you something — tell you all you want to know. There's no need of his guiding at all, only he likes it. I tell you what, sir, he's qualified for better things. He's—a—school—master!!!"

Of course we were overwhelmed, and engaged the schoolmaster at once, finding him a willing worker, a pleasant companion and an exceptionally good guide — thoroughly acquainted with the region through which we were traveling.

Four miles from Kellogg's we came to the rapids. Here the professor and myself took the loose articles, and the school-

CHARLEY BLANCHARD.

master started off with the inverted boat over his head, his shoulders fitting into the wooden yoke, on the ends of which the wales rested, looking like a huge inverted pickle dish on a pair of legs.

Reader, did you ever assist over one of these portages where, in the dense forests, the path seldom gets dry, and the decayed leaves and vegetable mould makes a bottom without a bottom, a river of black muck with roots and white stones projecting above the surface, which same are stepping places for the skillful but fearful traps for the unwary.

The guide takes the boat and you are expected to carry the lighter articles. You admire him as he starts out lightly, stepping from rock to rock along the slippery path. Your soul swells with conscious freedom, you snuff in inspiration and black flies by the mouthful, gather up the oars, paddle, guns, fish-rods, etc., and step out determined to show that you too are a natural woodsman. How exhilarating the action, the excitement of springing from rock to rock, watching your feet that they do not get the start of you, for the solid bottom may be anywhere from two

inches to two feet below the surface; dodging the bushes that scratch your hands and slap you in the face without the slightest provocation. After a while you find that the oars and other things are on a tender place, and you change only to make it worse; then they have got into a disagreeable habit of spreading out at various angles — straddling saplings, going on one side of trees when you had designed to pass on the

other, and when you back up for another start you wrench your neck, get a crick in your back in the struggle to dodge the various limbs that are making unprovoked lunges at you, and at last your foot glides gently down and disappears in the inky depths.

Surprise, perspiration and determination appears on your face as you plant the other firmly and making a desperate effort, resurrect the missing one with a *thuck* that nearly sends you over on the other side. Now, matters are getting interesting, and you, careless of results; the guide is disappearing through the trees, the things on your shoulder hurt worse and sprawl about more than ever, the young sapling and trees crowd closer to the path, and its like trying to push a cat through a knot-hole backwards. You look for all the world like a dilapidated umbrella sailing under bare poles, while your expression is any thing but that of a master of the situation as you put your foot down on one end of a dead root while the other comes up and swats you in the face with a dipper full of mud — the chances are that at about this juncture you begin to talk to yourself, it depends very much on how you were brought up.

Grimly you plow forward now, caring nothing how many trees you overturn in your course, determined not to back down for them at all events; then one on either side catch an oar, and they shut up on your aching neck like a pair of shears, a friendly limb lifts your hat and drops it in the mud right where you was going to step, so to save your hat you make some playful passes in various ways, one foot gets on top of the other, then they wander off in different directions and you sit down.

It is a delightful sensation to sit down — in the wild woods — after violent exercise — and rest. Gentle zephyrs steal refreshingly across your brow and black mud insinuatingly into your pants. At such a moment as this, free from the thraldom of civilization, in the solemn stillness of the mighty forests, with a soul attuned to the inspiring harmony of nature, your thoughts wander back to childhood's happy hours, and in the ecstasy of the moment some well-remembered passage learned at Sabbath-school comes welling up from your joyous heart. It is safest, however, not to let it well too much, as Bible quotations are liable to get somewhat mixed and a disinterested beholder might misconstrue your devotional expressions. At such an hour the most a man wants is undemonstrative sympathy — such episodes, however, are only the spice that season the dish of glorious things served up here among the mountains and lakes of the great wilderness.

A half-mile carry brought us to still water, then a short distance of boating to Buttermilk Falls, (which also lays claim to being Murray's "Phantom Falls!") Here the water dashes and foams down over the rocks, making a descent of about twenty feet, and the name, though not very poetical, was probably suggested by the churning that it gets in reaching the bottom.

"MURRAY talk about shooting the falls in his boat in pursuit of the phantom form, is a very probable story for a minister to tell," said the school-master with a contemptuous shrug. "It would sound better for one of us guides, though. Why, I drove a brood of ducks down over there once; the old one knew better than to go — she flew up stream — but they — a dozen of young ones — went over, and only three came out alive. *He* talk of doing it! There isn't Baptist enough about him, but there's one thing he *can* "shoot," that's the long bow;" alas for Mr. Murray's reputation for veracity — the beautiful creations of his fancy — the bright pictures conjured up by his fertile brain, are held as witnesses against him, simply because he, in his lavish generosity, enriched the common occurrences of every-day life in the woods with the precious increase of conceptive genius — leaving a dazzled world to separate the real from the ideal, and the guides take him literally as he says, and have come to the conclusion generally that if his preaching is not a better guide to heaven than his book to the Adirondacks, his congregation might manage to worry through with a cheaper man.

We put the boat in the deep quiet water above and went upward a mile and a half, then a portage of the same distance, brought us to Forked Lake.

FORKED LAKE is a lovely sheet of water about 5 miles in length, and appropriately named, as it is nearly all forks — a confusing train of alternate points and bays on the north, although on the south the shore is comparatively straight, the country being generally level or slightly rolling except where the Owl's Head looks over into the lake from the north-east. We passed the outlet of Raquette Lake and soon landed on the south shore at an old clearing, four miles from where we came in, where stood the blackened ruins of what was once a sporting house. Then through a half mile of cleared ground now overgrown with bushes, down into the tall timber land across the Carthage road, and we stood on the shores of

## RAQUETTE LAKE.

This, the "queen lake of the Adirondacks," is indeed a lovely sheet of water, lacking only the grand old mountains that some possess to make it all that heart could wish; it is over 1,700 feet above tide, surrounded by trees of almost every variety to be found in the wilderness, which stretches away in gentle undulations on all sides, with here and there a mountain ridge or peak rising above its fellows.

Where we first stood on the shore, the sombre pines lined the water edge and extended downward in inky shadows; toward the west, the portals widened out in successive shady coves, and bold rocky promontories, fringed with crimson maples, green and golden beeches, and the silver birch, while through these gateways, appeared gently sloping hillsides, edged with glittering sand that seemed to tremble in ecstasy under the heat waves of an unclouded sun.

Our course was westerly for a distance, then as we rounded a rocky promontory on the left and turned toward the south, a scene unparalleled for sweet, quiet beauty, burst on our enraptured sight. Behind us, across the glassy lake, a single boat was moving, leaving a double line of beaded silver to mark its course; beyond, from the north shore, a point came out, its surface almost as level as the motionless lake itself; edged with a smooth white beach, covered with grand old forest trees that ran up clear and straight for many feet, while upward through them curled the faint blue smoke of some hunter's camp fire. Now the shore sweeps around away to the west and comes back in the broad meadow and woodland of Indian Point, where once stood a village that has passed away, leaving only its name as the heritage of the red man; thence westward deep into Eagle Bay, and away toward the south, then approaching and receding in alternate wooded capes and deep bays to meet others on the east where the low ridges come down to the lake side, while between them the silvery water reflects island gems and vistas of tender purple distance.

The day, like the two preceding and the one to follow, was indescribably lovely; not a breath stirred the surface, nothing, save the Indian summer haze, which itself seemed luminous, dimmed the splendor of the sun's beams; the shore seemed to pass by us, a panorama of beauty — a constantly changing flash of gorgeous colors, sombre shade, gleaming sand, and a glittering edge of light that marked the line between the real and the reflected.

"Who would hesitate for one moment between the dusty city and a life among the grand old forests and lakes?" said the school-master. "How beautiful this free temple, where every thought is an anthem of praise and thanksgiving."

"Dem foin!" said the Professor, from the bottom of the boat, opening one eye a little way; "have you got such a thing as a sun shade or an umbrella about you?"

We spared him on account of his youth, but the school-master was sad — all his sentiment was crushed out of him — and when we asked who made the clearings around the border of the lake, of which we saw three or four with rude log houses built thereon, he said: "I don't know; some darn fool, I suppose, who expected to make a fortune here farming, forty miles from nowhere." They are all deserted now.

Raquette Lake has nowhere an uninterrupted water line of more than eight or nine miles, but from its outlet to Indian Point, then south through what appears to be a great irregular mass of bays and points, hanging to that side of the lake proper, to its head, is about twelve, but so irregular and winding its edges, that it is estimated to have a shore line of from 90 to 100 miles in extent. It contains a number of islands, the largest known as "Beach's," with an area of nearly 300 acres, is at the south end; it is covered principally with beech and maple, clean and clear almost as any park, and affords a delightful camping place for those so disposed. Another favorite, although one can hardly go amiss in selecting a camping place here, is now known as "Murray's Island," so named in honor of the reverend sportsman who usually pitches his summer tent here. The original and appropriate name was "Osprey Island," from a species of large bird who built nests and reared their young year after year in the great pines that stand there.

At the foot of one of these giants old Alva Dunning had built a bark shanty, and with his dogs lives there—a modern Robinson Crusoe. Two or three dogs came out with their master to see us—I cannot say welcome, for the dogs growled, and the old hunter growled, and our suddenly conceived idea of stopping there until the next day was changed by his surly permission when our desire was made known, so we continued on toward the east inlet.

Old Alva was in his normal condition—suffering from ill treatment. He has *always* been a sufferer, because he doesn't always look at things in the same light as others, and he believes to this day that it was only by chance, aided somewhat by an overruling Providence, that his life is spared, for did not Ned Buntline, the terrible, chase him all over Blue Mountain Lake with intent to deposit lead in his venerable cuticle? It is said that he hunted for Ned one summer and a misunderstanding arose, to settle which, Alva felt called upon to embezzle a boat of the novelist's, and after perforating it in various places to sink it in the lake. This manner of proceeding struck Ned as being out of order, so as a preliminary move he shot the old man's dog one day, while standing between his master's legs. This was nothing to the marksman, however, who is one of the best shots in the country, but Alva was grieved thereby, and threatened to set the "Eagle's Nest" on fire, with a longing to indulge in cremation. When asked about the affair, Ned said, "I drove him out of that section when I was there because he threatened my life. The old rip steered clear of me after he found that I was as ready to throw lead as he was *threats*."

It is said that the first house at Raquette Lake was built on Indian Point, then one nearly opposite by a Mr. Wood, who lived there about twenty years, became discouraged, and left. The old house still stands on the east shore, near Murray's Island. Near by is one of the loveliest lakes to be found anywhere in the region, known as Lake Eldom, a little more than a mile in length, about half that in breadth, and in shape, almost a perfect oval. It is reached from the main lake by a narrow stream through a wooded belt but a few rods in width, — claimed by some to have been the work of beavers. At the west end of the lake proper is the outlet of Shallow Lake, whose waters pass through Cranberry Pond and stream — a difficult route — to the Raquette. Into Shallow Lake empties that "nameless creek," where once, at sunset, "the air was literally full of jumping trout."

A small creek, known as the Brown Tract Inlet, empties in at the south-west point of Raquette Lake. Following up this for about four miles, then by a portage of 1½ more you enter the upper or eighth of the Fulton chain of lakes. Shed Lake and Mohican Pond is drained by the south inlet; Lake Fonda, the head-waters of the south branch of Moose River, can be reached in this direction by the river and two carries, of about two miles each.

There is but one hotel at Raquette Lake — that is "Cary's" — on the north shore near the outlet, where supplies are sometimes procured by fastidious parties who prefer a camp to the luxuries of a hotel.

MARION RIVER, often called the east inlet, is the largest feeder of the Raquette; toward this we turned the bow of our boat, and soon the quiet stream received us, shutting us in from the golden, queenly lake. Away to the east between the low hills that rise gently from the marsh on either side, Blue Mountain seemed to beckon us on; here the river is perhaps four or five rods in width, with an almost imperceptible current, hardly moving the lily pads that parted as our skiff scratched through the clusters, then drifted slowly back to their former position. This is a fair representative of a great many of the high country streams; deep, dark, still, covered with lily pads and bordered with a broad belt of reedy marsh. It is famed as a place for "floating," or Jack hunting, and we saw places where the ground was trodden by the hoofs of deer like that of a crowded sheep fold. For five miles the river was quiet, winding about so that, as the Professor suggested, "it would worry eels to follow;" then for another it rippled over sand and stones, where the overhanging alders slapped us in the face; then followed a portage of a half-mile —two and a half more of boating across Utowana Lake, a half mile or more through the dark woods with the yellow sunset sky at our backs for a guide, while the pedagogue took the boat up through the shallow brook into Eagle Lake and around to where we waited; then in the darkness we passed across to where a light shone out, and groping up the uneven slope found welcome and rest in the "Eagle's Nest," once the wilderness home of "Ned Buntline."

10

## CHAPTER X.

### "THE EAGLE'S NEST."

Where the silvery gleam of the rushing stream
Is so brightly seen on the rocks dark green,
Where the white pink grows by the wild red rose,
And the blue bird sings till the welkin rings.

Where the red deer leaps and the panther creeps,
And the eagles scream over cliff and stream,
Where the lilies bow their heads of snow,
And the hemlocks tall throw a shade o'er all.

Where the rolling surf laves the emerald turf,
Where the trout leaps high at the hovering fly,
Where the sporting fawn cross the soft green lawn,
And the crows' shrill cry bodes a tempest nigh—
  There is my home — my wildwood home.

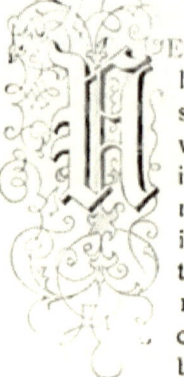

ED BUNTLINE, author of the above sweet lines that seem to rise upward like the joyous song of a wild bird, bringing thoughts of wild violets and the fragrance of dewy forests in its train, this strange man, with the blended natures of the tiger and the lark — the tender imaginings of a young girl and the uncontrolled passions of a wild beast — came here in 1856, that he might escape the dangers of civilization, and here had his alternate fierce battles and loving make-ups with his greatest enemy — the bottle. He gave the place and the lakes around the names they now bear; and lived here at odd times until the war cloud broke over the South, when his restless, venturesome nature called him to the field. Out of the war he came unscathed; but the end is not yet; whether it will be up through clearer paths to light, or downward with his life-long foe, cannot be foretold, while the great curse is left to blacken the land.

But the old eagle has flown, other birds of prey occupy the nest, and a brood of young ones gathered around, climbed on us, counted our buttons, pulled our hair, and made us generally welcome, and the way we went for the food set before us would have made ordinary birds of prey tremble for their reputation. This, the only house in the locality, affords a comfortable stopping place for sportsmen through the summer months, and for lumbermen during the winter. A gang of these hardy sons of toil came in while we were there, took their supper, and when we thought they were fairly settled for the night and were apparently going off in a nice snooze, those men of Belial got up, knocked around the furniture and stove, rattled pots and kettles until the rooms were full of steam and the air of frizzled pork and profanity, then away to the woods, whence with the first gray streaks of morning light, came the sound of their axes and the crash of falling trees. When river driving commences, they often stand all day long soaked with the ice-cold waters that come down from the melting snows above, and only constitutions of iron can endure what they do at times, but as a class they are careful not to tax their strength by any needless intellectual pursuits, such as poring over newspapers or books in the glare of unhealthy burners or any thing of the kind, and by their abstemious habits in these respects, many are enabled to earn from two to three dollars per day through the season, and endure it for eight or ten years before they become too stiff to move. EAGLE LAKE is the middle link of the Eckford chain, very

"NED BUNTLINE."

pretty and about one mile long. At its east end the boat is pushed or towed up through a narrow channel from which the stones have been removed; here the road from North Creek, 30 miles distant, crosses, parties sometimes entering the wilderness from this direction, but the condition of the road for half the distance is such that it is not very popular at present.

BLUE MOUNTAIN LAKE,

Or Lake Emmons, is called the gem of the smaller lakes, it is three miles in length, very irregular, especially along the west shore, and contains a number of picturesque islands, some of them mere rocks, rising above the surface, while others are covered with trees of various kinds. It is also sometimes called Tallow Lake, because of an old Indian who mourned a canoe load of venison tallow with which he once started for the distant settlement. Alas! the wind blew, the treacherous waves engulfed it, and the noble *Grea*sian paid Deer for his temerity. On the east rises Mount Emmons, commonly called Blue Mountain, from the color which is popularly supposed to pervade it, and enters into nearly every picture of this region.

We had reached this, the head waters of the Raquette, and

rested on the west beach, 35 miles as we had come and only 5 miles from where we left Long Lake, but between it and us was a mountain carry of three miles, not generally liked by the guides. The schoolmaster decided the question of which route to take back by shouldering his boat and starting up over the mountain. The path was very good — a gradual ascent for some ways, then a long reach of swamp and open meadow land where the springy surface of matted grass and interlaced roots, shook and bent over unknown depths of black muck that oozed up along the slippery stepping places and mingled with the snow of the week before which still remained, then we descended the north side of the mountain into the forest-embowered waters of South Pond, a row of 1½ miles took us past the comfortable looking shanty of A. F. Tait and to the outlet, there a portage of another mile to Long Lake, and by boat to Kellogg's, where we astonished the proprietor by the earnest manner in which we devoted ourselves to business at the dinner-table.

After dinner we chartered a seat in a farmer's wagon and went to "Aunt Polly's" to spend the Sabbath with its genial proprietor, John Davis, where Mrs. Davis loaded our plates with broiled venison, partridge, trout and other good things, until we were forced to cry enough, even after riding over that road in a lumber wagon. This old established hotel, long and favorably known as "Aunt Polly's," is on the main road, 14 miles from Long Lake and 22 from Minerva; stages pass twice, weekly, through the sporting season, usually stopping over for the night.

A new route lately opened up and growing to be a popular one, is by boat and carry through a lovely chain of lakes and ponds to the "Island House," on Davis Island at the foot of Long Lake, 12 miles distant.

MOUNT JOSEPH, a curious freak of nature, and one well worth a visit, is six miles from Davis', and presents every appearance of being an extinct volcano, only in place of the yawning crater is a lovely little pond 50 rods in diameter, said by some to have a depth of 80 feet, while others tell of vain attempts to fathom its waters; it is, indeed, a curious sight, a vast spring on the very summit of a mountain, 1,200 feet above tide.

## CHAPTER XI.

### "On the Tramp."

THUS far our travels had been principally by carriage of some kind or by boat. We had been almost around the great peaks but not among them. The mountains that now looked down on us from the north we had viewed from the other side; passed around to the west along up Long Lake; made a loop of over 40 miles in the trip to Blue Mountain and back, then east to Newcomb; now, we must trust to our feet to carry us over the route laid down, and thanks to the pure air, and our initiatory struggles over the various carries, we felt equal to the task, so on Monday morning, with knapsacks strapped on our backs, we started for Adirondack, the ruined village among the mountains, eighteen miles distant.

Soon we saw an old friend, the Hudson River, on whose bosom floated the wealth of nations, here so narrow that in places we could almost jump across it. From the north it came, moving sluggishly along between the dark balsams that lined its banks and extended, an apparently unbroken forest, for miles back, while away over beyond rested the faint blue crest of Tahawas, "the cloud-splitter." Six miles from "Aunt Polly's," the road divides, the south branch going to Minerva, and the other to the lower works, 2 miles distant, thence east to Root's hotel, 19 miles further.

"TAHAWAS," so called on the maps and in the postal departments, is generally spoken of here as the "lower works," to distinguish it from the upper Adirondack village; once there were extensive buildings at this place; a long dam across the

Hudson, here called the North River, flooded the valley back to the outlet of Lake Sanford, and heavy barges floated between carrying provisions up and bringing ore down. Now the dam is gone, the old kilns are in ruins, dead trees mark the flat where the waters once stood, and there is, I think, but one family there, excepting those occupying the hotel, a large white house with comfortable accommodations for 20 guests, but aside from its interest as a hotel, is the fact that it is the home of John Cheney, "the mighty hunter" of the Adirondacks.

We stopped for dinner, partially to see the old man, and partially because we felt a peculiar sensation stealing over us — an indescribable something that had attacked us regularly three times a day of late. In answer to our summons, a young man appeared in the doorway, of whom we asked if we could have dinner.

"I dunno," said he. After a suitable time given to silence, the subject was again advanced in the way of an assertion. " W-e w-o-u-l-d l-i-k-e s-o-m-e *dinner!*"

The smile increased in sickly strength, and it was evident that he sympathized with us — sympathy is good, but it won't sustain life. We made another effort:

"Can we have dinner?"

He laughed a little, said "fifty cents," then he laughed a little more and rested at a half smile ready to go off at the slightest provocation. I looked at the Professor and did not wonder that the young man had misgivings as to his intentions, the Professor looked at me and was not surprised that the pleasant youth was in doubt as to mine. Time had passed lightly over our heads without improving our clothing in the least. I tried another tack:

"Is Mr. Cheney in?"

"Guess not, hah."

"Where is he?"

"Gone huntin', guess."

"Mrs. Cheney?"

A flickering smile seemed to admit that that fact could no longer be concealed.

"We would like to see her."

"Fifty cents—dinner—hah."

"But I want to see Mrs. Cheney."

"Can—spose—hah."

With a withering look at the Prof, whose dilapidated appearance had undoubtedly brought us into such a plight, I started on a tour of discovery and found Mrs. Cheney flying around, preparing a dinner for us, having evidently seen us coming and concluded, by our looks, that we needed something—which we soon had, and while enjoying it, she, in a pleasant, cheery sort of way, talked about her absent husband.

He was born in New Hampshire, June 26, 1800, living there and at Ticonderoga until 30 years of age, when finding that game was growing scarce, he shouldered his rifle, and calling his faithful dog, set out for the then almost unknown wilderness. For years he lived alone on what his gun brought him, and ever since, his life has been that of the hunter. Many stories are told indicating his coolness in times of danger, his skill and daring as a hunter, and an account of his perilous adventures would fill a large volume. Headly, the historian, saw him when he first visited this region thirty years ago, and speaks of him as having "none of the roughness of the hunter, but as one of the mildest, most unassuming, pleasant men to be met with anywhere." Mrs. Cheney said he had gone hunting with some of "the boys," "for" she continued, with a flash of pride, in her sense of ownership, "if he *is* 73 years old, he can run in the woods now and beat most any of 'em when he feels like it; if you could see him and he happens to feel all right, you could find out a good deal, but he's awful changeable, either awful good or awful bad." We did not see him, but in reply to a letter, received the following in a firm, readable hand :

\* \* \* "I've always had a great love for the woods and a hunter's life ever since I could carry a gun, and have had a great many narrow escapes from being torn to pieces by bears, panthers, wolves and moose, and many a time I have had to put a tree between myself and an enraged bull moose. After a while, finding a rifle unhandy to carry, I had a pistol made expressly for my use. The stock was made out of a birch root, the barrel was eleven inches long and carried a

LAKE SANFORD.

half ounce ball, and is now on exhibition at the Geological rooms at Albany. I received one hundred dollars for it after

it was pretty nearly worn out. Once I was rowing after a large buck deer, when it was accidently discharged, the ball striking me about half way between my knee and ankle, came out on the other side just below my ankle joint, but being 14 miles from any habitation and alone, I only stopped long enough to see what harm it had done, then seized my oars and started for him again as the thought struck me, I may need that deer now more than ever. I caught up with him and made short work of it, took him ashore, dressed and hung him up, but I soon perceived that if I ever got out of the woods I must lose no time, as my boot was full of blood and my ankle began to pain me very bad, so I cut two crotched sticks, and by their help managed to get out of the woods, but it took me about eight hours; I only stopped to set down once, it was so hard to start again.

I could tell you lots of my adventures if I could see you, but find I must stop writing as it would take all the paper in the house to write one quarter of them."

Accompanying this was a photograph of the old hunter — a venerable looking face set in a framework of silvery hair and beard — bearing a kindly look over all, even though the eye had a severe expression — caused undoubtedly of that blawsted photographer who is continually stirring a body up by sprightly commands to "look pleasant."

From the lower to the upper works it is ten miles over a passable road running north along the west side of the valley; Half way up, the foot of Lake Sanford is reached, where boats can be taken if desired, although the best way, if not desirous of fishing, is to continue along the road. The lake is four miles long, the shores low and marshy, looking more like a broad river than a lake, as it rests between the hills on the west, and North river mountain on the east.

Just above the head of Lake Sanford is the "new forge," the huge building itself in a dilapidated condition, but the great stone furnace, forty feet square at its base, stands firm and solid as when made; a few rods beyond this is the ruined village, where a scene of utter desolation met our view.

ADIRONDACK.

Nearly a quarter of a century has passed away since the busy hum of industry sounded here; where once was heard the crash of machinery and the joyous shouts of children at play, is now the shrill bark of the fox or the whir of the startled partridge; in place of the music of voices, all was silence, solemn and ghostly. Over the mountains and the middle ground hung a dark funereal pall of cloud across which the setting sun cast bars of ashen light; they fell on the nearer buildings bringing out their unseemly scars in ghastly relief and lay in strips across the grass grown street which led away into the shadow. On either side once stood neat cottages and pleasant homes, now stained and blackened by time; broken windows, doors unhinged, falling roofs, rotting sills and crumbling foundations, pointed to the ruin that must surely come. At the head of the street was the old furnace, a part of one chimney still standing, and another shattered by the thunder bolt lay in ruins at its feet. The water-wheel — emblem of departed power — lay motionless, save as piece by piece it fell away. Huge blocks of iron, piles of rusty ore, coal bursting from the crumbling kilns, great shafts broken and bent, rotting timbers, stones and rubbish lay in one common grave, over which loving nature had thrown a shroud of creeping vines.

Near the centre of the village was a large house said at one time to have accommodated one hundred boarders, now grim and silent; near by at the left stood the pretty school house; the steps, worn by many little feet, had rotted and fallen, the windows were almost paneless, the walls cracked and rent asunder where the foundation had dropped away, and the doors yawned wide, seeming to say not "welcome" but "go."

> "O'er all there hung a shadow and a fear,
> A sense of mystery the spirit daunted,
> And said as plain as whisper in the ear,
> The place is haunted."

As we advanced a dog appeared at the side of the house and howled dismally, then, as if frightened at the sound of its own voice, slunk away again out of sight. We knocked at the door, but no sound save a hollow echo greeted us from within; that was also deserted. Then we went out in the middle of the street where, suspended in a tree, hung the bell that used to call the men to work, and on the Sabbath, perhaps the villagers to worship in the little school-house near by. Clear and sweet, pure and fearless, its tones rang out over the forests, away to the mountains, then back to us dying out in soft echoes, and with it went the cloud that had oppressed our spirits.

Once more we knocked at the door of the large house, invited ourselves to enter, and, passing through the sounding hall, made our way to the back portion of the house, which bore signs of having been recently occupied, foraged around until we discovered that there was no danger of immediate starvation, then built up a fire and set about preparing our evening meal.

Just then voices sounded outside — the door opened and a lady stepped lightly inside. Was it a phantom form such as Murray saw? Apparently not, for her garments were more sensible and better adapted to life in the woods; she did not appear surprised in the least to see us there, and, as she did not seem inclined to apologize for intruding, we concluded that it was our place to do so, and began, but were stopped by the remark that we did right, the door was never locked.

Soon Mr. Moore came in; a general introduction followed and we were made welcome in true backwoods style " to such fare as they had," which, as it consisted of delicate steaming biscuits, the sweetest of butter, fragrant tea and other "fixins," was good enough for a king — and it is altogether likely that if the king had been there the independent Californian would not have considered it worth his while to offer him anything better than he did us.

That night we listened to stories of hunting and trapping, of mountain trails and forest paths, wonderful stories about the chasm of the Opalescent, the wildest gorge in the country, where for two miles the river foams and thunders over successive falls, one fully seventy feet in height, through rifts in the solid rock, five hundred feet in depth and scarcely eight feet across at the top; of a line of traps sixteen miles long, which the little woman who welcomed us should tend, making her rounds on snow-shoes, when the time for them came, *alone;* think of that ye city weaklings as you take your airings on soft cushions, and then wonder if a life among the mountains is beneficial. When Mrs. Moore came to the woods she was brought in by her husband an invalid; now, with him, she roams through the forest and mountains, goes hunting, fishing and *guiding*, when there are ladies to accompany the parties.

"We came here to hunt and fish, wife and I, and the less people come the better it will please us," said John Moore, as we were leaving in the morning, "but if people *will* come, we will try and take care of them in the proper season; it is past that now, so you can put up your money, I don't want it." Then we left the couple who cared for no society, save their own and the wild, free forests, with a friendly feeling in our hearts and the major part of two chickens in our knapsack — we needed them before we got through Indian Pass.

The old village is in the midst of wild and picturesque scenery; just a little way north is Lake Henderson; from the head of this a trail leads to the Preston pond, the head of

Cold river; Lake Harkness is one mile distant; Lake Andrews, specially noted for its quantities of trout, two. Toward the northeast to Calamity pond, it is four miles; to Lake Colden, six; Avalanche lake, seven and a half; to the summit of Mt. Marcy, twelve miles.

The history of the place is brief and sad. In 1826, Messrs. Henderson, McMartin and McIntire had iron works at North Elba. One day an Indian showed them a piece of ore of remarkable purity, which he said came from a place where "water run over dam, me find plenty all same."

The services of the Indian were secured at once, at the rate of two shillings and what tobacco he could use per day, to conduct them to the place spoken of. Equipped for a long tramp they started, and on the second day arrived at the site of the present village, where they found, as the Indian had said, where the water literally poured over an iron dam. Hastening to Albany, a large tract of land, embracing the principal ore beds in that vicinity, was secured, forges, etc., built, operations commenced, and a road cut from the lower works to Lake Champlain. Mr. Henderson always had a nervous terror of fire-arms, and on the day of his death his pistol was in the pack carried by his Guide, who laid it down to perform service required of him. Thinking that it had fallen in a damp place, Mr. Henderson picked it up and dropped it on a rock near by; with the motion came a sharp report from the pistol, the hammer of which had probably struck the rock in falling. Mr. Henderson fell to the ground, saying "I'm shot," and soon breathed his last. The hunter Cheney was with him at the time, and tells a pitiful story of the grief of the little son, who was also along. The body was borne out on the shoulders of workmen, and afterward a beautiful monument placed where he fell, bearing the inscription: "Erected by filial affection to the memory of our dear father, David Henderson, who accidentally lost his life on this spot by the premature discharge of a pistol, 3d Sept., 1845." The place has since been called Calamity Pond.

The whole enterprise had been financially a failure. In the death of Mr. Henderson the motive power was removed, and it was allowed to run down, work gradually ceased, and three years after his death the upper works were abandoned; the lower ones were soon after left, and at last all that remained of the noisy village was an old Scotchman and family, who took care of the property and took in strangers that chanced to come that way, myself among the number.

Well do I remember the night when they sent us to sleep in one of the deserted houses having the reputation of being haunted. We did imagine that we heard curious sounds during the night, but whether uneasy spirits or some poor dog that we had robbed of his nest we could not tell. We quieted our fears and consciences, however, with the reflection that if it was a ghost, it would never think of looking for human beings in *that* bed, and if a dog, he certainly hadn't lost any thing worth mentioning in the operation.

LAKE COLDEN is two miles from Calamity Pond, and six from the village. Here the Marcy trail should be left and time given to one of the wildest water views in the mountains, which is reached by a rough trail of two miles toward the north.

AVALANCHE LAKE is high up among the mountains, 2,846 feet above tide, its waters like ice and its walls of black rock running down deep under and up perpendicularly hundreds of feet on either side. It is half a mile in length, and but a few rods wide. Between it and Lake Colden are two immense slides that descended the mountain long before the place was known, and are now covered with a heavy growth of timber, supposed by some to have caused the little lake by imprisoning its waters in the narrow defile.

In 1867 an avalanche of loose rocks and earth swept downward from the summit, and carrying everything before it plunged into the sleeping lake below, nearly dividing it in two. This, the latest of any note, can be followed up to near the summit, but cannot be left without the aid of ladder or ropes. Where it started it is but eight or ten feet broad and as many deep, but increasing in volume as it dscended, it tore its way through the soft rock until, at the bottom, the track is 75 feet wide and 40 or 50 deep.

Here in 1868 occurred a pleasant little episode in which " Bill Nye took a hand," which we wish to remark is not the

Bill Nye who had that little affair with an innocent celestial, but William B. Nye, a noted guide and hunter of North Elba.

"Bill," as he is familiarly called, is one of those iron-moulded men just turned fifty nearly six feet in height, powerfully built, knowing no danger or fatigue, and well versed in woodcraft. Silent, morose even if you in any way gain his dislike by a display of supposed superiority, (and by the way, he is but a type of the old time guides who, as a class, are modest, unassuming and withal, as noble a set of men as walks the earth — who have learned their own insignificance among the grand things of nature and silence in her solitude; who know what is becoming in man, and the upstart who presumes too much on his position as employer, expecting fawning servility, had better go back to civilization for all the extra comfort he can get out of a sojourn in the woods.) If he likes you he cannot do too much for you, always ready and willing, and around the camp fire his tongue once loosed, the stories of wild wood life told in his quiet quaint style is full of interest — and a sure cure for the blues.

"Come Bill — how about that adventure of yours at Avalanche Lake?" said one of the party gathered around the blazing fire. We all had heard of it, but wanted the facts from the principal actor.

"What adventure?" said Nye.

"Oh, come, you know what one we mean; go ahead." So, after considerable innocent beating about the bush to ascertain the one meant, although it was perfectly evident that he knew all the time, Nye told his story:

"Well, boys — some of you may remember a party of three — Mr. and Mrs. Fielding and their neice, from somewhere or other on the Hudson, that I went guiding for in 1868. Mr. Fielding, was rather a little man, one of those quick motioned, impulsive sort, who make up their minds quick and is liable to change it in five minutes afterward, but a very generous gentleman withal; his wife was taller and heavier than he, would look things carefully over before she expressed an opinion, and when she made up her mind to do a thing she did it; the neice — Dolly they called her — was about seventeen years old, a splendid girl, handsome as a picture, and she knew it too, all very sociable and willing to talk with any one; and I tell you boys, when I look at such a girl I sometimes feel as though may be I have made a mistake in living alone so long, but I'm too old a dog now to think of learning new tricks, so we will go on."

"Well, our trip was to be from Nash's through Indian Pass to the iron works, then on to Mount Marcy and back by way of Avalanche Pass. We got rather a late start from Nash's, and all the boarders told Mrs. Fielding she could not go through that day. She says 'you'll see I shall, if the guide will show me the way.' She *did* go through, though she traveled the last three or four miles by torch-light. I tried to have her let me build a little camp and stay till day light, she said 'No; you know what they said when we started, if you can find the way I am going through.' I told her I could find the way if it was darker than a stack of black cats; she says, 'lead on, I will follow.' The last mile she carried her shoes in her hand, but she *beat*, and that was enough. The next day we went to Lake Colden and camped; the next to Mount Marcy and back to Colden camp again.

The following day we started to go through Avalanche Pass to North Elba — you will remember the walls, hundreds of feet high on either side, that you can neither get over nor around without going around the mountain, well, along one side is a shelf from two to four feet wide and as many under water, and when we got there they wondered how we were to get past. I said I could carry them or I could build a raft, but to build a raft would take too much time while I could carry them past in a few minutes. Provisions were getting short and time set to be at North Elba, so Mr. Fielding says, "Well, Matilda, what say you? Will you be carried over, or shall we make a raft?" Mrs. Fielding says: 'If Mr. Nye can do it, and thinks it safe, I will be carried over, to save time.' 'Well, Dolly, what do *you* say?' 'Oh, if Mr. Nye can carry aunt over he can *me*, of course; I think it would be a novelty.' Mr. Fielding says: 'Well, we have concluded to be carried over, if you can do it safely.' I said "perfectly safe; I have carried a man across that weighed 180 pounds, and a nervous old fellow, at that.' I waded across and back to see if there had been any change in the bottom since I was there before. When in the deepest place the water is nearly up to my arms for a step or two; I had nothing with me then. When I got back Mrs. Fielding said she did not see how I was going to carry them across and keep them out of the water. I said 'I will show you; who is going to ride first?' Mr. F. said 'it was politeness to see the ladies safe first; so *Matilda* must make the first trip;' *she* would 'let the politeness go, and would like to see Mr. F. go over first,' but he said 'she had agreed to ride if I said it was safe; *now* he wanted to see her do it;' 'and *so I will!*' said she; 'how am I to do it?' I set down with my back against a rock that came nearly to the top of my shoulders, told her to step on the rock, put one foot over one side of my neck, the other over the other side, and sit down. *That* was what she did not feel inclined to do, and was going to climb on with both feet on one side, but her husband told her to 'throw away her delicacy, and do as I told her,' reminding her of her word, which was enough; she finally sat down very carefully, so far down on my back that I could not carry her, I told her it wouldn't do, and at last she got on and I waded in.

"'Hurrah! there they go!' 'Cling tight, Matilda!' shouted the young lady and the husband in the same breath. 'Hold your horse, aunt!' laughed Dolly. 'Your reputation as a rider is at stake; three cheers for aunt Mazeppa!—I mean aunt Matty; novel, isn't it? Unique and pleasing; you beat Rarey, auntie, that's what you do!'

"I had just barely got into the deep water, steadying myself with one hand against the rocks and holding on to her feet with the other, when, in spite of all I could do, she managed to work half way down my back.

"'Hitch up, Matilda! *hitch up*, Matilda! why *don't* you hitch up?' screamed Mr. Fielding, and I could hear him dancing around among the rocks and stones, while I thought Dolly would have died laughing, and the more he yelled 'hitch *up*,' the more *she* hitched *down*, and I began to think I would have to change ends, or she would get wet; but by leaning way over forward, I managed to get her across safe and dry. Then 'how was she to get off?' I said, 'I will show you.' So I

"HITCH UP, MATILDA."

bent down until her feet touched the ground, and she just walked off over my head, the two on the other side laughing and shouting all the time.

Then came Dolly's turn; I told her that she must sit straight as a major general; she said she would — she'd let them see that all the money spent at riding schools hadn't been thrown away in *her* case. Wondered if any poet would immortalize her as they had Phil. Sheridan; then with some kind of a conundrum about Balaam (I never thought much of conundrums anyway) she got on and I took her over and unloaded her the same as I did her aunt. The rest was easy enough, rather more in my line too, and we got back all right. Of course I did no more than my duty at the time, but you can bet I kept pretty still about it for some time, until at last it leaked out; but there is one thing I would say, the ladies never told of the adventure or made the slightest allusion to it in public as some would, in my presence at least, and for thus showing so much regard for the feelings of a bashful man and a bachelor I shall be grateful to them to my dying day."

LAKE HENDERSON is about two miles long; its outlet near the centre on the east, about half a mile north of the old iron works; through this break we see the high peak of Colden, and the track of the Avalanche from summit to base gleaming like snow in the sunlight; the beauty of the shore is somewhat impaired by dead trees that line them, but it is withal a beautiful sheet of water. Mountains stoop down to it on all sides, on the west is seen Sandanona, Henderson and Panther Mountain — its base laved by the deep waters; while on the north we can look up a gradual slope through grand old Indian Pass, with the dark green sides of McIntyre on the right and mighty Wall Face on the left, rising almost perpendicularly over 1,300 feet from the trail below. Pulling to the head of the lake in a boat, of which there are several as safe as the one Noah built, we took to the woods accompanied by a brother of Mrs. Moore's, who kindly offered to start us on our way, and followed up along the east side of the rapid stream that came from the notch above.

# CHAPTER XII.

### Indian Pass.

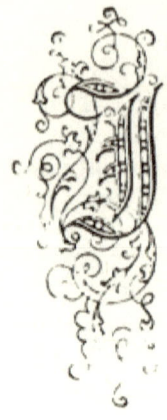I HAD expected to find a level, fertile, grove-like way through which we could walk with little exertion in the shadow of great rocks on either side, but how different the reality; for three miles the rise was gradual, then we began to climb, crossing the rivulet back and forth as we went upward, at times making long detours to the right and ascending the mountain some distance, then a level stretch along its sides until the wildly dashing torrent was reached once more; then onward, upward, the path growing wilder and more difficult, the brooklet bounding from rock to rock, then lost in some dark cavern, anon trickling down among the huge boulders, gurgling in muffled music beneath our feet, then bursting out to rest a moment in some mossy basin, pure crystal in an emerald setting on which floated fairy ships of Autumn leaves, then onward in its long journey to the sea.

We had caught occasional glimpses through the trees of — was it a cloud or solid rock that rested off toward the left, we could hardly tell until we traced its outline against the sky, for Indian summer had hung her mantle of haze over the great cliff and it seemed but a shade or two deeper than the blue above. At last, through an opening it came out; vast, grand, overwhelming, immeasurable. The eye saw it hanging in mid-air, a cloud, an outline, a color; tender, sweet, luminous. The soul felt and bowed beneath its awful weight. The giant pines that fringed its brow seemed bristling hair, the great rifts and seams a faint tracery that scarred its sides. Motionless, it still seemed to be sweeping grandly away as clouds shot upward from behind and passed over to the east, then approaching, and re-

INDIAN PASS.

treating, as cool gray shadows and yellow sunlight raced swiftly across or lay in slant bars along down its misty face.

But the highest point was not reached yet; we were just entering at the lower gate, and for nearly a mile it was a continuous climb over great chaotic masses of jagged rock, thrown there by some convulsion of Nature, now on a huge fragment that seems ready to topple over into the gulf below, now under a projecting shelf that would shelter a large company, now between others from which hang dripping mosses and sprawling roots, stooping, crawling, clinging to projecting limbs, climbing slippery ledges, upward all the time.

The trees that had found lodgment on the top of the rocks seemed to reach out thirstily for something more than they found in their first bed; one that we noticed had taken root on the top of a huge boulder, and sent down a mass of interwoven roots twenty feet to the damp earth beneath.

At last we near the summit and stand on Lookout Point; close by rises that grand wall a thousand feet up, and extending three hundred feet below us, reaching out north and south, majestic, solemn and oppressive in its nearness; a long line of great fragments have fallen, year by year, from the cliff above and now lie at its foot; around on every side huge caverns yawn and mighty rocks rear their heads where He who rules the earthquake cast them centuries ago. Along back, down the gorge we look, to where five miles away and 1,300 feet below us is Lake Henderson, a shining drop in the bottom of a great emerald bowl.

Slowly the sun swung around toward the west, the shadow of the great wall crept down into the valley across the gray rocks, and over toward the mossy ones that had lain there unnumbered centuries; gradually the sweet tinkling, gurgling music of the infant Hudson died away and solitude reigned. Then as we passed onward a familiar sound came once more, faintly at first, then more distinctly, the singing of little waters; first trickling over rocks, then dancing downward, increased in volume by tributary streams from the slopes of McIntyre — rocked in the same mountain cradle, twin brothers and equal at their birth — the mighty Hudson rolling southward, and the impetuous Ausable dancing away toward the north. Down the rocky bed of the stream we went until we had left the pass behind, through the thick pines and hemlock out into hard timber land, our only guide the blazed trees, for the leaves covered the ground like a thick carpet, often hiding the slight trail. Over the foot hills of the mountain on the west, often misled by seeming paths until the absence of scars on the trees warned us to retrace our steps and gather up the missing thread. On and on, until it seemed that the eighteen or twenty miles we had expected to travel before seeing a familiar landmark had lengthened out into twice that number; then in the gathering twilight we emerged from the woods in sight of North Elba, forded the Ausable — grown to be quite a river since we had left it away back toward its head — and up to Blin's, with a sound as though a whole colony of bull-frogs were having a concert in each boot.

Does it pay to go through Indian Pass? I answer a thousand times yes. It costs a little extra exertion, but the experiences and emotions of the day come back in a flood of happy recollections, and the soul is lifted a little higher and made better by a visit to that grand old mountain ruin.

MOUNT COLDEN.    McINTYRE.    INDIAN PASS.
[South from Blinn's.]

SCOTT'S, a mile east of North Elba, is an old stand well known to the traveling public. It is advertised as a good point to start from for Indian Pass and other points of interest. We took dinner there and came to the conclusion that it *was* a good place to start from. That afternoon we went east, ten miles, to Keene, thence south, to the Flats, but as they are usually entered by way of Elizabethtown, we will, if you please, glance at that route.

## CHAPTER XIII.

### PLEASANT VALLEY.

LEAVING the steamer at Westport, an enjoyable stage ride of eight miles takes us through a notch and out where we can look down in that lovely mountain-guarded retreat known as Pleasant Valley, scarcely less beautiful than its twin sister Keene Flats over across the grand ridges to the west, save that the mountains do not crowd against it quite as closely and look down on it from less giddy heights; like the other it is a favorite resort for the artist, the quiet lover of Nature, and ladies, whose protectors, made of sterner stuff, are away in the mountains and lakes of the west.

ELIZABETHTOWN, the picturesque little village at our feet, is the county seat of Essex, contains a population of fifteen hundred; three churches — Methodist, Baptist and Congregational — four or five stores, three hotels, county offices, court-house, jail and an unlimited number of lawyers. One would hardly imagine it, lying so peacefully in the valley below, but such is the fact. It has produced some of the brightest legal lights of the age, and is at present the home of a number of prominent men, among them Congressman Hale, Judge A. C. Hand and others; it is also the old home of Hon. Orlando Kellogg, who was returned to Congress by a grateful constituency term after term, until the day of his death — an honest politician and a noble man.

The village is very quiet and orderly, is peculiarly an American town, with no foreign population, and no mills or forges to fill the streams with sawdust, your clothes with soot, or your eyes with cinders.

Of hotels, the Valley House, in the business portion of the village, is spoken highly of, and will provide for from forty to fifty guests.

THE MANSION HOUSE, Simonds & Kellogg, proprietors, is designed more especially for summer boarders. It is situated on the upper level at the southern edge of the village, a large white three-story building, with a verandah running on three sides, ceilings high, rooms large and well furnished, and will, with the two cottages connected with it, accommodate two hundred guests. See page 172.

Mr. Simonds is a veteran hotel man, with an experience here of over a quarter of a century. Until quite recently he kept the Valley House, then feeling that a wider field was opened by the crowds of city people who began to flock to Pleasant Valley, he, with Mr. O. Kellogg, opened the present fine hotel, which has become a very popular summer stopping place.

COBBLE HILL, a little way toward the south-west, is a bold craggy mountain front, rising like a huge pyramid apparently right up out of the plane at the end of the road. "OLD HURRICANE" is the highest peak near by; a sharp cone on which the sun seems to hang as it bids the valley good night. A wagon road leads to its base five miles distant, from which by a sharp climb of two miles the summit is reached, giving one of the finest high views to be obtained in the Adirondacks, said to some to be second only to that of Whiteface.

Toward the south the mountains approach each other, growing rough and precipitous as the level interval narrows down, at places breaking off suddenly in perpendicular walls a hundred feet in height, at others, rounding over in great, nobby, boulder-like masses to the level that flows along their base almost as evenly as though it were water instead of the fertile bed of a valley.

Eight miles from Elizabethtown is Split Rock Falls, where the water comes sparkling and foaming down through a gorge and over the rocks, descending about a hundred feet, then takes its quiet way along toward the north.

Euba Dam is, or rather was, the name of a little place two miles further, but as its use had a tendency to familiarize the youth of the land to incipient profanity it was changed to Euba Mills.

Six miles, over a rather road, is Deadwater, appropriately enough named, for the few weather-stained buildings are almost worthless. North Hudson is four to five miles farther, and Root's famous old hotel-stand, two miles beyond that. From Root's to Schroon Lake is about nine miles. North of Elizabethtown the road runs through close under the frowning ledge of Poke-o'-Moonshine, and out across the plain to Keeseville, twenty-two miles distant. To the west it winds up over the mountain pass between Old Hurricane and the Giant, through a wonderfully picturesque drive to Keene, eleven miles, westward, by the lovely Edmonds' ponds, at the base of Pitchoff Mountain, out across the plains of North Elba, with its grand panorama of mountains at the south — to Lake Placid and the Saranac, making undoubtedly the nearest and most picturesque route to the lakes to be found in any direction.

A FOGGY MORNING IN CAMP.

"Where *did* we put them?"

# CHAPTER XIV.

### Keene Flats.

KEENE FLATS undoubtedly possesses the loveliest combination of quiet valley and wild mountain scenery in the Adirondacks, if not indeed on the continent. Through it, from the south, come the sparkling waters of the Ausable, here flowing quietly along beneath overhanging maples and gracefully swaying elms, there rippling over glistening white sand; now murmuring through pleasant meadow-land, anon dancing away among the stones; then dashing down rocky raceways to where, among the spray and foam of the cataract, it thunders and rumbles and roars as if angry with its prison walls; then onward between the dark overhanging ledges outward through the northern portals and away to join its sister from the great Indian Pass above.

A little way south of the falls the road from Elizabethtown comes in on the east, south of this we follow up the stream that winds quietly along through the Flats from its head six miles above. Soon some of the beauties that have lent such a charm to this locality begin to appear; we see sweet, restful shady, groves of water maples, great massy drooping elms, clumps of alders fringing the river brink, great canopies of native grape-vines clasping the huge rocks in loving embrace or festooned on the sturdy trees through which open up long vistas of meadow-land, a back-ground of mountain green, and above all, summits of glittering granite.

On every side they shut us in, rising right up out of the Flat instead of the gradual curve of a mountain from the plain, showing that the bottom of the lovely valley is but the accumulated deposit of long ages, where the floods swept down from the mountains and left their sediment in the notch below.

Through the gradually raising break in the mountains toward the west, Mount Marcy looks over into the valley, and there near its summit is the head of John's Brook, which joins the Ausable where we stand. On the east, among the group that surround the giant another brook rises, and the water foaming down the sharp descent plunges over Phelp's Falls and joins the river a little below.

T. S. Perkins, it is said, was the first artist to find his way in. Coming in 1857 and when he went out it was with sketches of surprisingly lovely scenery found in a spot hitherto unknown among his fellows. The following year brought others, and soon, through their paintings, the world learned of this quiet little nook, and the appreciative lovers of nature found their way there. Now, there are a number of wealthy people owning summer places, and during the season almost every farm-house is full to overflowing.

THE TAHAWUS HOUSE is the largest in Keene Flats; a roomy comfortable looking structure, with a broad two story piazza, and has accommodations for about forty visitors. Its proprietor, N. M. Dibble, seems to have learned the secret of success in that line, and has made his place very attractive in its clean, well ordered appearance; it is very much liked by former guests; teams are furnished for the pleasant drives north and south, and to meet parties at Westport when desired. (See page 173.)

From this central position the outlook is very beautiful, taking in the grand mountains as you swing slowly around, and the lovely river moving onward toward the north. Along the west side is a level table land extending almost the entire length of the valley, beyond this is one of the Ausable or long pond group, locally known as the west mountain; on the east side is Baxter mountain, one thousand feet high, generally called the Balcony, as from its edge the entire flats seem to lie like a garden spread out below; directly opposite our lookout point is Spread Eagle Mountain and Hopkins Peak still farther away. Toward the north-east is the fire blackened sides and sharp cone of Hurricane Peak; over the near mountains to the south-east the giant lifts his craggy head, and in the south on either side, Mount Dix and the Ausable Mountains are piled up in broken masses against the sky, while in the centre is the graceful gray outline of the central beauty among the grand mountain sentinels — Dial Mountain — the " noon mark " of Keene Flats.

The streams and cascades, easily accessible from the flats, are too numerous to mention, too wild and varied to be described; they must be seen to be appreciated, either with a guide or by making systematic exploring expeditions in various directions, where rare wonders and glorious surprises await the earnest lover of nature.

E. M. CRAWFORD, a little way north of Dibble's, has a very pleasant place; the house nearly new; newly furnished with especial reference to the wants of summer visitors, and will take care of 25 to 30 guests; the jovial proprietor has traveled east somewhat, has learned eastern ways and customs, and may be expected to treat his company in the squarest manner possible; like Dibble, he furnishes horses when desired, is considerable of a hunter himself, and as wholesouled gentlemanly a fellow as you often meet. Besides those mentioned there are others prepared for summer company. Hull's, near the entrance; Washbond's, a little south of Dibble's; still farther the Dr. Potter place; then the Widow Beede's, and the house of Smith Beede — a noted guide — at the head of the Flats.

We reached Keene from North Elba late in the afternoon, entered the gateway with the last rays of the sun crimsoning the eastern mountains, passed up along the valley in the golden twilight, and as night came down around us, drew up at the hospitable door of the Crawfords. I say " drew up," for at Keene we fell in with a resident of the Flats, a genial, cheerry old boy, whose nature is like his name, and whose age entitled him to hair of the same color; he insisted on going considerably out of his way to be sure that we went right in ours, and when we bade him good night, asking how we could repay him, he said, " Now dont you say nothing more about that, mebby you can do some one else the same good turn sometime." Then he drove away back through the darkness, as merry as a cricket, and we went inside.

Mr. Crawford was away on a hunting expedition. Mrs. Crawford was indisposed that evening. The boys, though willing, were weak, and the help had gone with the summer company, so, for a few minutes, the prospects of a hot supper looked dubious, but as every crisis brings to the surface some master of the situation, ours appeared in form of the accomplished wife of an eastern artist who did the honors of the establishment in a mountain costume, and with a completeness that could not have been improved, joining heartily in the repast herself and leaving the mind of one of her guests at least, in a vague misty sort of wonder at the rather pleasant mixture of flaky biscuits, golden butter, fragrant tea, apple blossoms, pearls, oat meal, rosebuds corn bread, sparkling eyes and cheeks the very picture of health, and *she* came to the woods an invalid. Is the free pure air of the mountains and forests good? Try it and see.

ORSON SCHOFIELD PHELPS is what his parents named their baby, and "Old Mountain Phelps" is what every body calls him now; but his first name was given 57 years ago, sometime before he had earned the last. He was born in the Green Mountain State, from which he came to the western part of Schroon when 14 years of age; he had an enthusiastic love for the woods, took to them on every possible occasion, and was a long time engaged in tracing out wild lot lines that extended far in the interior, "where in those times, deer and speckled trout were as plenty as mosquitoes in a damp day in July." He doesn't aspire to much as a hunter, but claims to have caught more trout than any other man in the

"OLD MOUNTAIN PHELPS."

country. In 1844 he was with Mr. Henderson at Adirondack, soon after which he married and settled in Keene Flats, and in 1849 made his first trip to the top of Marcy, passing out over Haystack around the head of Panther Gorge and to the summit, descending near where the main trail now runs, being the first man to get to the top from the east; he afterward cut what is now known as the Bartlett mountain trail, and soon guided two ladies up, which was considered quite a feat for them to perform and a feather in his cap, as it had been considered impracticable until then. He also marked trails to the top of Hopkins' Peak, the Giant, up John's Brook to Marcy, and several others; has made a valuable map of the country around, is a prized and regular contributor to a local paper, and has written a voluminous treatise on the Adirondack lakes and mountains, trees, birds, beasts, etc., which shows the close observer and enthusiastic student of nature, and which will contain much valuable information when, as is promised, it is given to the public.

We found him at his home near the falls that bear his name — a little old man, about five foot six in height — muffled up in an immense crop of long hair, and a beard that seemed to boil up out of his collar band; grizzley as the granite ledges he climbs, shaggy as the rough-barked cedar, but with a pleasant twinkle in his eye and an elasticity to his step equaled by few younger men, while he delivers his communications, his sage conclusions and whimsical oddities, in a cheery, cherripy, squeaky sort of tone — away up on the mountains as it were — an octave above the ordinary voice, suggestive of the warblings of an ancient chickadee.

"So you wanted old Mountain Phelps to show you the way, did you?" said he, "Well, I s'pose I kin do it. I'll be along as soon as the old woman'll bake me a short-cake. The wise man provides for an emergency, and hunger's one of 'em." So we returned to Crawford's for breakfast, after which, when the old man appeared with his little hatchet and big provision bag on his back, Mrs. Crawford had her nettlesome ponies brought around, and, with the artist's wife, carried us all up to the Widow Beede's, where we bade them good-bye, delighted and duly grateful for the breezy ride of the morning.

At the head of the Flats the Ausable from the south-west and Roaring Brook from the south-east join ; between them is the Widow Beede's place. When we reached the summit of the hill, back of the house, we saw a lovely view of the valley and the mountains on either side, stretching away for twenty miles toward the north and south.

" ROARING BROOK comes mostly off of that," said Phelps, pointing to the east where the "Giant" lifted his scarred and rifted head high up in air. "You see that chasm there ? That is the lower end of Russell Falls. There is a gorge through that hill near 200 feet deep, the width of the river, and nearly perpendicular walls on either side, a continuous ragged fall all the way for half a mile, at no place more than 25 feet at one leap, but there is a great variety in them ; when the water is low you can go through, but it isn't nice going at the best."

" See that bare rock near Smith Beede's ? There are Roaring Brook Falls, the highest in the mountains ; nearly 200 feet sheer fall at one leap, and I tell you it isn't much besides spray when it reaches the bottom ; a mile above that — you see where Roaring Brook comes down the side of the Giant, through that dark ravine — there is Chapel Pond, just northeast of it is another one, nearly as large, that's called the "Giant's Wash Bowl," a narrow rim of rock only holds it in on the lower side, which is so steep that you can stand on its edge and throw a stone down into Chapel Pond, eight hundred feet below.

RESAGONIA or Sawtooth Mountain appears in the southwest, its curiously serrated crest gaining it the title also of Rooster's Comb. East of this is a round, rocky knob, known as Indian Head, and over this, a little further east, is a sharp peak called Mount Colvin, after the superintendent of the Adirondack survey, who is supposed to have been the first man on its summit. Between the two mountains that drop downward at an acute angle, lies the lower Ausable Pond, four miles distant. Toward this notch we took our way down a little hill into the woods and up along brawling Gill Brook, over a path that is sometimes dignified by the name of wagon-road, but over which but few would attempt to ride.

"All things is possible and nothing ompossible," said Phelps, diving into the bushes on one side of the road, and soon reappearing with a piece of band iron which he stowed away in his bag. "like as not I will need this to mend an oar or something; old Phelps is such an easy old critter to get along with, that they take his boat, bang it 'round as much as they want to, maybe break an oar, and *he* never'll make a fuss about it; shouldn't wonder a bit if they had it off somewhere now."

MT. COLVIN, AUSABLE PASS, KESAGONIA.

After what seemed a long four mile tramp through the woods, we came out in a little opening near the brow of a hill, and were just rising to look out when a fierce gust of wind from the other side set the old man's hat whirling back toward us; we succeeded in spearing it, then as we turned and glanced out ahead, were surprised, almost dazzled by the wonderful beauty of the scene that flashed out so suddenly and unexpectedly on our astonished sight.

AUSABLE POND in all its Swiss-like beauty was before us. We stood at the end of our road on the brow of a hill whose front had apparently been undermined, and ran sharply down to the water's edge, gleaming, drifting, unstable sand. On the left, close by, was old Indian Head, the side toward us all in shadow: rough and jagged, standing like some grim sentinel to guard the narrow pass at his feet — beyond was Mount Colvin, the sides rising in places straight up from the water, then backward to the sharp ridge nearly 2,000 feet above, seemingly crowned with a coronet of diamonds that flashed and glittered as the water trickled down over the rocks, and reflected back the sun's bright beams. On the west was Resagonia, almost as abrupt, although trees grew from its sides close down to the water's edge; between them the narrow Pond stretched away, its head hidden by the point on the right, its outlet at our feet.

RAINBOW FALLS is across the outlet to the north-west, back in the gorge, you can see where the brook starts, away up on the Gothic Mountains, and trace its course down the steep side until it is lost at the base. We crossed the outlet and went up into the cleft mountain side, very like Ausable Chasm and probably with a like origin. It extends only a short distance but is very beautiful, the gray sides perpendicular for something over a hundred feet, while huge rough boulders fill the bottom, and over the edge of the wall at the north is the Fall, a skein of amber silk that flutters along down the rocks until whipped and ravelled, it reaches the bottom as lightly as a snow-flake falls and white as clean wool, where, gathering its tiny drops together, it goes softly singing down its emerald-paved steps to the river below.

We descended to the outlet, where we compelled Phelps' shortcake to assume an indisposed sort of expression. then taking a boat started up the Pond, over which the wind swept fiercely, picking up the crests of the racing waves and dashing the spray in our dripping faces, while the old man pulled and talked, as though getting wet was the natural and happy culmination of the very enjoyable trip.

The Lower Ausable Pond is something over a mile in length, but a few rods wide, and in the very heart of the mountains, at the same time one of the lowest and easiest passes through them, providing always that a boat is found in which to pass this point, for the rocks on the east come down so straight into the water that it would be impossible to get past there, and the west shore is almost as bad, although by some rough climbing among the huge masses that have fallen from the rocks, a person may succeed in passing safely. Toward its head the water "shoaled" until it came above the surface, a strip of natural meadow, and gradually rising, was covered first with bushes then with a growth of heavy trees as though not the water alone but the soil that fills this trough of the mountains was passing slowly, like some great glazier, toward the plain.

From the head a walk of a mile up along the brook, brought us to the shores of the Upper Ausable, where Phelps expected to find his boat. "Just as I expected," said he, finding matters as he had anticipated, "Old Phelps' boats belong to everybody but himself, well we haven't got much farther to go to my shanty, that's one satisfaction, and maybe they'll let us stay there all night, considering that it belongs to me." So we skirted the west shore a little way and came out at the shanty, where we found Crawford's party jubilant over the fourth deer they had taken in three days, and preparing supper to which we did full justice.

GOTHIC MOUNTAINS.

THE UPPER AUSABLE POND is nearly two miles in length and perhaps a half mile wide, it is noted hunting ground as deer started in the mountains around, if not too far away, usually make for this water. There are two or three good log shanties on its shores, and a number of boats here and at the lower pond owned by the Keene Flat guides.

On the east is the Boreas Mountain, a long ridge terminating in Mount Colvin at the north, and extending south for ten miles. At the west is quite a high ridge called Bartlett Mountain, upon which the shortest trail goes to the top of Mount Marcy, 5 miles distant.

Beyond Bartlett is the Haystack, a sharp cone-like granite peak standing about fourth or fifth in height; over beyond it the summit of Marcy, 5,333 feet above tide; toward the north and east comes Basin, Saddleback — one of the .win gothics — Resagonia and the notch where lies the lower pond, a grand circle of giants, rifted and scarred, upon whose sides we can mark the course of mountain torrents and the white glistening path of the avalanche. The shores of the pond are thickly wooded to the water's edge (excepting here and there a break where are the camping places) and so level toward the south for a little way, that it is said in times of flood a boat can be pushed over into the Boreas waters, whose outlet is the Hudson.

The ascent of Marcy is oftenest made from this direction by leaving the upper Ausable pond near its outlet, passing up over Bartlett Mountain to Marcy Brook, three and a half miles distant; then up toward the west or through Panther Gorge, but we can not do better than give the trip in the words of the "old man of the mountains," who stands ready to relieve us, so we will stand aside and give him the floor.

Ladies and gentlemen — Mr. Phelps:

"Well, I guess I kin show you the way, fur I've been up there near a hundred times, I 'spose. Let's see, we're in Panther Gorge now, I believe, and before we go up Marcy, I want to show you a sight up here from the side of Haystack that is worth seeing, where we can look right down into the gulf below. See that precipice on the Marcy side? It is one continuous wall of rock a mile in length, circling around to the head of the gorge with Castle Column at its head; that is one of the wildest places in the Adirondacks, where, after a heavy rain or in the spring, streams pour down it from all sides You see that water-course over there in the centre? I have seen an almost unbroken sheet of water, six feet wide, pouring over that to the bottom of the gorge, almost a thousand feet below. Now we will pass on up the trail once more, just stopping to notice those shafts of rock across on the Haystack side. There are three of them, entirely detached from the wall near by, about ten feet square, and one of them near fifty feet high, with a loose cap-stone on top of it. The soft rock must have crumbled away between them and the main ledge while they were left standing. Now, out at the upper end and we begin to climb Marcy, striking the John's Brook trail that goes down to Keene Flats near its centre. Up here, on the side of the mountain, we find a little marsh, which is the head of the longest branch of the great Hudson River, and the largest branch of the Ausable; but our trees are getting stunted and we will soon be able to see over the tops of them; it's about like going through a thrashing machine trying to get along before they are chopped out; but here we are at last at the top, and you see this is the place to see things; down there at Marcy Brook, where we turned to go through Panther Gorge, comes the other trail up this way, running spirally up the south side from east to west until it strikes the smooth rock that has been swept clean by the avalance; then up that, across back and forth to its head. It is about as steep as the roof of a house, and when it is wet and slippery it's bad getting along, but when its dry it sticks to your boots like sand paper. In making the round trip the trail goes down the north side a ways to the head of the Opalescent, then west through the valley and out by Lake Colden and Calamity Pond to the Adirondack Iron Works.

The summit of Tahawus is comparatively level for 6 rods north and south, and 15 rods east and west, a few loose boulders lie about promiscuously. At the west end of this flat is a mass rising up some eight or ten feet that contains the highest solid rock in the State of New York. Tahawus has something of a ridge-like appearance, running north-east and south-west, although its whole formation is a comparatively round mound of rock. The upper thousand feet is bare, and clear the farthest down on the south-west side; the west side of this mountain has more the appearance of a pasture hillside than a mountain above vegetation, its partial covering of Alpine grasses and other plants and shrubs give it a domestic and agricultural appearance. The whole south side is covered with bristly balsam up within a few rods of the top, and is the steepest and longest side, sloping away 1½ miles at the rate of 2,000 feet to the mile, to the foot of Panther Gorge. Large portions of the south side have been swept off by avalanches, the east is far the roughest part of the mountain, it drops off the first thousand feet about its average incline among broken cobbles and gulches, and then takes one final leap of 1,000 feet into Panther Gorge. The Panther Gorge trail passes up through this, and is the easiest grade to the summit. On the north side it drops down to the head of the Opalescent valley, more or less broken with precipices and ravines. The Adirondack trail passing np this side over cliffs and bluffs that are next to impassable. This mountain, as well as all others that rise above vegetation, has a belt of the stunted balsam.

To the north, over a mass of wild mountain ridges, we see the cleared fields of North Elba, Lake Placid and the western slope of Whiteface, beyond that the St. Regis and Chateaugay woods.

Turning slowly to the north-east we see Table-top Mountain and the mass of mountains about it, and the extensive mountain range that lies between the two branches of the Ausable, in which is Slide Mountain, also John's Brook Valley and Keene Flats and Hurricane Mountain; over beyond is the Broad Lake with Burlington on the eastern shore. Still turning, we see the avalanche rent mass of the Gothic Mountains, the Giant, Hopkin's Peak, and over among the Green Mountains, Camel's Hump; and, still farther, the dim outlines of the White Monntains. East is Haystack and Saw-teeth Mountains, the lower Ausable Pond, Mount Colvin, the Dial, Camel's Hump. East south-east, is the Boreas Mountain, Nipple-top, Mount Dix, and a host of others. South-east is Bartlett Mountain, upper Ausable Pond, Boreas Range, Mud Pond, Clear Pond, Macomb Mountain, and a mass of hills from that to Lake Champlain. South south-east your eyes follow down the deep valley of Marcy Brook to the broad marsh and swamp above the Ausable Pond to a full view of Boreas Mountain; passing over that comes Blue Ridge and the nameless mass of mountains and hills about Schroon Lake and Lake George, of which Black Mountain is very prominent. South you look obliquely down Marcy Brook on the west side to Moose Mountain, Boreas and Wolf Pond; in the south-west is Skylight, Mount Allen, Cheney Cobble,

North River Mountain, still further is Blue Mountain, Raquette Lake and the John Brown Tract; while Mount Redfield, Lake Sanford, Lake Delia and Mount Goodnow is west south-west. West, the view drops down to little Lake Perkins (or summit water, 4,293 feet above tide, the true high-pond source of the Hudson River), then over a broken, ragged mass of mountains to Mount Adams and the upper Adirondack iron works, Lake Henderson, Santanonia Mountain and the Owl's Head; while a few points toward the north we look over Lake Colden, Calamity Pond, Preston Ponds Pass, Mount Henderson, Gray Mount, and over the lower mountains to Cranberry Lake region. North-west is Mount Colden, Mount McIntyre, the Opalescent Valley and Colden Ridge; beyond, old Wallface and Mount Seward, and between these the dark Oulusca Pass the *place of shadows* of the Indian.

In the many times and days I have been on its summit, I have but three times had what I call a first-class clear view, then I could see the outlines of two of the summits of the White Mountains in New Hampshire, which must be at least 150 miles distant. It is a fair view to see the outlines of mountains 60 miles. I once saw the clearing up of a thunderstorm at sunset; there was a tornado sweeping over the top of the mountain and the fog-clouds, broken into patches, were running at lightning speed, and when one of those clouds would strike the mountain all would be shut in with fog for perhaps two or three seconds when it would open, giving a view to the west of a dazzling brilliant orange-tint over the whole western sky. This could be enjoyed from two to four seconds more when the enveloping fog would come again to save one from going crazy, I suppose. The sun appears over the Green Mountains, in July, eight minutes before sunrise by the almanac, and is in sight seventeen minutes after sundown.

A thunder storm in the night is an awful sight from the summit of Tahawus. I once saw one at near midnight, approaching from the west, when it was all below me, and I could look on the top of the cloud and see the streaks of lightning darting in every direction; it appeared like a mountain of serpents writhing in every conceivable manner. When it finally reached me, it appeared very natural, with the exception the thunder seemed very near by. There are a great variety of fog scenes; I saw one of three-fourths of the circle about me, a level ocean of fog and the other quarter clear; it made me think of a big pie with one quarter taken out; another one was of fog driven over Skylight in a bright moonlight night, it pitched over the east side like a mammoth water-fall, which it was, not of a river but a cloud; another majestic sight was the gathering and passing up of what we call a quick south storm; when I first saw it, it was some forty miles distant, coming on at the rate of a mile in two minutes; a massive cloud with the driping curtain of rain reaching down to the earth; as it passed up nearer it threw out some of the most wonderful shades and colors; in the centre it was of a clear gray; some six to eight miles to the east and west, of a bright purple, growing lighter to the extremes, and to the east and west softening down to a sunshine hazy light; it passed over to the St. Lawrence lasting near two hours.

"STORIES."

CAMP PHELPS, on the upper Ausable, is one of the most complete in its appointment and management of any shanty in the Adirondacks. The structure is of an elegant design, and built of magnificent logs cut and curved artistically with knots of various and unique patterns in bas relief. The main door is about 2½ by 5 feet, swings outward, and is locked with a string; it contains an immense reception room, drawing room, private parlor and sleeping rooms *en suite*, with wardrobes sticking out all around the sides. The grand dining hall is situate out on the lovely lawn, which is quite extensive, and splendidly furnished with hemlock extensions and stumps. This spacious structure is six by ten feet on the ground, and between four and five feet high, and is surmounted by a Yankee roof of *troughs* in two layers, the upper covering the crevices in the lower so as to exclude the rain, but separated far enough to give perfect ventilation. This *chef d'œuvre* of architecture is first class in every respect, it is luxuriously upholstered throughout with spruce boughs, in the culinary department is a stupendous range which floods the drawing room with light, and, in short, it contains all the modern improvements, including hot and cold water, which is carried to every part of the establishment in pails. Here we gathered, Crawford's party of seven, and ours, ten in all, beside two or three dogs, in a space about six by eight feet square, and while the fire snapped and flickered, filling the shanty with dancing shadows, stories of hunting and fishing adventures were told that all were expected to believe because they were personal experiences, although occasionally one would have a familiar sort of sound with the exception of names and dates. Stories of personal prowess which culminated in one of a man who could pick up a two barrel iron kettle by the edge with his teeth, and the assertion by another that he knew a man who could perform the same feat sitting in the kettle himself when he lifted it, which was making light of serious subjects, and so Phelps told his bear story, how one day near the Boreas, he saw a big bear coming on the run after him and he, armed with only a little ax, then when the bear got within twenty feet of him he yelled "halt," which stopped the bear — he couldn't prevaricate, he did it with his little hatchet — he didn't feel scared any, only stirred up like, but the bear reversed ends and made off as fast as it could wabble. Then Uncle Harvey told all about how he killed a bear with a pitchfork once, and a moose with a club, after tiring him out in the deep snow. "But, by gawl, boys," said he, "When Dick Estus tumbled over backward on his snow shoes, and the critter gave a lunge for him, I thought it was all up with him, but I just gave command to the boys, and at him we went, and, by gawl, the way we laid it on his old hide was a caution, and there lay Dick, square on his back, looking up, thinkin' that every minute was his last, and, by gawl, I just managed to get a lick at the critter that fetched him just as he was standin' over Dick so," and the old hunter assumed a position, indicative of an enraged moose preparing to come down on an unfortunate little chap on his back in the snow, who couldn't turn over on account of his snow-shoes. Thus each had their stories to tell until time to turn in, when four of the party went across the pond to another camp, leaving six of us to occupy a space six feet long by six feet wide, and where we slept on edge, like a box of well-packed sardines, until daylight, when each man got up and cut a chunk of venison, salt pork or bacon as taste dictated, and each man for himself waltzed around that stove in the six by ten shanty until he had warmed it through enough to suit, or disguising pieces of raw material in an outside coating of bread, proceeded to stow it away with that appearance of keen enjoyment displayed by the average boy in taking a pill; then a part rushed away to put out the dogs, others to the various runways. The old man gave his attention to some sort of a stew, which, as he had made no calculations on staying out all night, and the camp supplies had run low in the particular materials needed, was partially a failure; the professor, with a home-sick sort of expression on his face, was picking away at an ancient piece of bacon, while an enthusiastic individual who had wallowed in an ecstacy of imaginative bliss, theoretically, over venison stake, broiled at the blazing camp fire, was engaged in preparing a savory strip of the same, which as he forgot to apply salt, and got hold of a piece just moderately warm—not cooked, at the first bite, roused a rebellious feeling within him, and he felt the full force of those saddest of all words, "it might have been done," but it was not ordained to be, and at last, as his mind kept running on accounts of ship-wrecked people who had to eat each other or starve, and cannibalism seemed imminent, one of the guides came in like a dove bringing—not the olive branch exactly — but a bag of oat-meal, which he made into pan-cakes, and those pan-cakes went to our hearts and stomachs like the blissful ecstacy of love's young dream. We were saved, and while we ate he baked and brought them forward; none of your little patty-cakes, but great big ones the size of the frying pan, and as light as sea foam almost, making, with maple sugar, a breakfast, the which when suggested, makes my mouth water to this day, and the more we ate the happier he seemed to feel about it; thus casting his bread upon the waters; a little act of simple courtesy perhaps, offered without a thought of return; but it showed the willing, generous disposition, and those pan-cakes touched a chord in the breast of one individual at least that will vibrate for all time, and if he is ever permitted to go there again he would not ask for a more willing assistant or, if reports be true, a better guide than Theo. White of Keene Flats, the author of those glorious pan-cakes.

After breakfast Phelps took us up the inlet, with its dark borders of balsam and tamarack, to the Marcy trail, where, bidding him a regretful adieu, for we had become attached to the cheery old man of the mountains in our short acquaintance, we started on our tramp of sixteen miles, out through the woods to Root's, feeling that we were nearing friends who would be glad to welcome us home; clearer in thought and stronger in body than when we entered; glad to go back but sad at thought of leaving the mountains, over which we saw the storm-cloud gather, break and roll away, leaving them, — kissed by the loving sunshine, clean, grand, strong and eternal as the hand that made them.

## CHAPTER XV.

### Guides.

GUIDES receive from $2.50 to $3.00 per day furnishing boat, with every thing usually required for camping purposes, and doing all the work, although employers are expected to assist with the lighter articles over carries.

The following lists were furnished by the several gentlemen to whom credit is given, and supposed to contain the names of all actively engaged in the profession at the places mentioned. If, however, any have been omitted or mistakes made in those given, the publishers will consider it a favor to be notified of the fact, and the corrections will be cheerfully made in future editions.

It were useless attempting to give rules for selecting a guide, or to discriminate between those mentioned, they are, *as a class*, a noble set of men, who feel themselves the equals of their employer, and, to a great extent, reflect back their usage; there are, of course, exceptions to the rule among guides as there often is among employers. If you ask only reasonable service there can usually be no complaint; if you expect fawning servility the prospects are that you will soon be without a guide, for one who knows enough for the profession knows when he is well used; experience only can lead to a satisfactory solution of the problem; neither is this list intended to designate the particular locality to which they are competent to guide, as many are familiar with the entire wilderness, but to give their post-office address and be a reference table to those who desire such an one.

## St. Regis Guides.

Paul Smith gives employment to a large number during the season, and furnishes the following list of those who make his house their headquarters. Their post-office address is Bloomingdale, Essex Co., N. Y.:

George Martin, Fred. Martin, Doug. Martin, Henry Martin, John McLaughlin, Frank Hobert, Moses St. Germain, Ben. St. Germain, Levi St. Germain, Bonum St. Germain, Nelson St. Germain, Fayette St. Germain, Joseph Newell, Lovel Newell, Sylvester Newell, Thos. Redwood, Moses Sawyer, Emon Jaquish, John Hall, Lias Hall, F. Baker, Zeb. Robear, Sr., Zeb Robear, Jr., Ed. Robarge, Steven Turner, Sim. Forence, Elverdo Patterson, James Patterson, Gard. Maloney, Ben. Monty, Eugene White, Jacob Stayes, Ross Stayes, Ahas Stayes, Warren Flanders, A. C. McCollum, Oren Otis, Myron Otis, John Otis, Sylvester Otis, Fred. Otis, Henry Chase, Ben. Munsil, Henry Kent, Loney Moody, Phil. King, James Cross, Charles Dwight, Fred. Barnes, James Bean, A. Norton, Seth Wardner, John Wake, Henry Weller, M. Labrake, E. J. Noyes, Geo. Butts.

## Saranac Lake.

William F. Martin, himself a noted hunter and guide, now proprietor of the Lower Saranac Lake House, furnishes the following:

Stephen C. Martin, John Solomon, John Grover, Benny Moody, William Moody, Ed. Flagg, George Wake, Mark Clough, Joseph Hanmer, Carlos Whitney, Ed. Otis, A. W. Duelley, R. W. Nichols, George H. Ring, John King, James Philbrook, Fred. Reynolds, Edward Brown, Hosea Colbath, Albert P. Robbins, Albert McKenzie, Charles Greeno, Sem. Corey, Lucius Evans, F. G. Hallock, Richard Moody, Fayette Moody, Marshall Brown, George Sweeney, D. S. Moody, James McClellan, Alric Moody, Chester McCaffrey, J. Otis, Jason Vosburgh, Wm. E. Ring, Henry Douglass, Reuben Reynolds, Ransom Reynolds, George Mussing, John Benham, Henry Wood, Charles Greenough, John Slater, Charles Corey, Charles Hikock.

Post-office address: Saranac Lake, Franklin Co., N. Y.

# GUIDES.

BARTLETT'S—Clark Farmer, the Coreys, Daniels, and others who live near the Upper Saranac, are addressed as above. For the Tupper's Lake Region apply to Martin Moody—same address.

## LONG LAKE

is noted for a number of superior guides of the kind called independent. C. H. Kellogg, Esq., of the Long Lake Hotel, has furnished the following list:

Mitchel Sabattis, John E. Plumbley, Reuben Carey, Nelson Carey, Charley Blanchard, Reuben Howard, Jerome Wood, Jeremiah Plumley, Charles Sabattis, Isaac Sabattis, Henry Stanton, George B. Stanton, B. F. Emerson, Amos Robinson, John Robinson, William Robinson, Isaac B. C. Robinson, Att. Cole, Simeon Cole, Lysander Hall, Herbert Hall, John Rice, W. D. Jennings, C. D. Hough, George Cary, William Helms, David Helms, David Keller, C. R. Keller, C. B. Hammer, Alonzo L. Mix, David Mix, Gilbert Stanton.

Post-office address Long Lake, Hamilton Co.

## NEWCOMB.

Thanks are due to Mr. John Davis of the Halfway House for the following list:

Washington Chase, Franklin Chase, Jefferson Chase, Caleb I. Chase, Elis C. Chase, Adelbert Parker, John F. Far, Charlie Far, Jr., Nelson Bissle, Charles Bissle, Joseph Bissle, Willie Alden, James Hall, Henry H. Snider, Ozias Bissell, Harrison Hall, Alonzo Wetherbee, Henry Parker, M. R. Sutton, James Bissell, William M. Aldin, Valorous Hall.

Post-office address Newcomb, Essex Co., N. Y.

David Hunter, David Cheney—Post-office address: Tahawus, Essex Co.

## ADIRONDACK IRON WORKS.

John Moore—Post-office address: Tahawus, Essex Co.

## KEENE FLATS, ESSEX CO.

(Post-office address as above.)

O. S. Phelps, Harvey Holt, E. Phelps, Max Tredo, Levi S. Lamb, Munroe Holt, Smith Beede, Hiram Holt, Orlando Beede, Theo. White, Byron Esles, Will Tredo, Melville J. Trumbell.

### NORTH ELBA, ESSEX CO.

The following guides may be engaged through either Nash or Brewster at Lake Placid, or by letter as above:

Wm. B. Nye, George Billings, Peter Aldridge, Ed. Smith, Peter Lamoy, Edwin Kenney.

### WHITE-FACE MOUNTAIN.

(Post-office address: Wilmington, Essex Co.)

V. Mihills,          M. F. Hays,          E. D. Hays.

If your point of operation is decided on, with which you are as yet unacquainted, it is best to leave the matter of procuring a guide entirely with your prospective landlord, stating what you want, remembering that the best guides are usually engaged some time in advance. Some parties attempt occasionally to get along without regular guides by aid of maps, compass and books, but at the best that is very uncertain — is full of hardships that are easily avoided by those accustomed to the country, and if distance, comfort and time lost in out-of-the-way places are taken in consideration, attended with but little economy.

EXEUNT GUIDES.

# CHAPTER XVI.

## ROUTES.

### Route No. 1.
#### NEW YORK

| | Miles. | | Miles. |
|---|---|---|---|
| To Sing Sing | 32 | To Glens Falls | 204 |
| West Point | 51 | Whitehall | 223 |
| Poughkeepsie | 75 | Westport | 278 |
| Rondout | 90 | Port Kent | 313 |
| Catskill | 111 | Plattsburgh | 328 |
| ALBANY | 144 | Rouse's Point | 353 |
| Troy | 151 | Montreal | 403 |
| Saratoga | 182 | Quebec | 583 |

### Route No. 2.
#### ALBANY

| | | | |
|---|---|---|---|
| To New York | 144 | To Fort Edward | 55 |
| Troy | 7 | GLENS FALLS | 60 |
| Cohoes | 9 | Fort Ann | 66 |
| Junction | 12 | Comstock's | 70 |
| Mechanicville | 18 | Whitehall | 77 |
| Round Lake | 25 | LAKE STATION | 79 |
| Ballston | 31 | Castleton | 90 |
| Saratoga | 38 | Rutland | 101 |

### Route No. 3.
#### WHITEHALL

| | | | | | |
|---|---|---|---|---|---|
| To Benson | | 13 | 13 | To Westport | 11 | 55 |
| Orwell | | 7 | 20 | Essex | 10 | 65 |
| Ticonderoga | | 4 | 24 | Burlington | 15 | 80 |
| Larabee's | | 2 | 26 | Port Kent | 10 | 90 |
| Crown Point | | 9 | 35 | Plattsburgh | 15 | 105 |
| Port Henry | | 9 | 44 | ROUSE'S POINT | 25 | 130 |

### Route No. 4.
#### ROUSE'S POINT

| | | | | |
|---|---|---|---|---|
| To Montreal | 50 | | To Chateaugay | 17 | 45 |
| Boston | 289 | | Malone | 12 | 57 |
| Mooers | 12 | 12 | Potsdam | 47 | 94 |
| Dannemora | 16 | 28 | OGDENSBURG | 34 | 128 |

### Route No. 5.
#### CHATEAUGAY

| To Falls | Miles. 1 | To Upper Lake | Miles. 14 |
| Lower Lake | 8 | Head of Lake | 19 |
| Narrows | 11 | | |

### Route No. 6.
#### PLATTSBURGH

| To Point of Rocks.. | 20 | 20 | To Martin's | 7 | 55 |
| Ausable Forks .. | 3 | 23 | Dannemora..... | 16 | 16 |
| Franklin Falls .. | 17 | 40 | Chazy Lake..... | 5 | 21 |
| Bloomingdale ... | 8 | 48 | Upp. Chateaugay | 6 | 27 |
| Paul Smith's ... | 10 | 58 | Lower Lake..... | 6 | 33 |
| Martin's ........ | 8 | 56 | R. R. at Chat'gay | 8 | 41 |
| Whiteface Mt. H. | 30 | 33 | Ausable Chasm.. | | 12 |
| Wilming'n Notch | 6 | 39 | Montreal........ | | 74 |
| North Elba . ... | 6 | 45 | Boston ......... | | 260 |
| Lake Placid .... | 3 | 48 | New York ...... | | 328 |

### Route No. 7.
#### KEESEVILLE

| To Burlington ......... | 14 | To Martin's ............. | 45 |
| Plattsburgh ......... | 13 | Paul Smith's ......... | 47 |
| Port Kent .......... | 4 | Whiteface Mountain.. | 22 |
| Ausable Chasm ...... | 2 | Wilmington Notch... | 28 |
| Point of Rocks ...... | 9 | North Elba ......... | 34 |
| Ausable Forks ....... | 12 | Lake Placid......... | 37 |
| Franklin Falls ....... | 29 | Martin's ............. | 44 |
| Bloomingdale ........ | 37 | Elizabethtown ....... | 22 |

### Route No. 8.
#### "ROUND TRIP."
#### MARTIN'S

| To head Saranac L., | 6 | | Over Big Clear Pond | 2 | 25 |
| By River........... | 3 | 9 | Portage ............ | 1½ | 26½ |
| Across Round Lake, | 2½ | 11½ | Upper St. Regis L. | 1½ | 27¾ |
| To Bartlett's ....... | ½ | 12 | Thro' Spitfire Pond | | |
| Head Upper Lake.. | 8 | 20 | and Creek to Paul | | |
| Carriage .......... | 3 | 23 | Smith's........... | 2½ | 30 |

# ROUTES.

### Route No. 9.
#### WESTPORT

|  | Miles. |  | Miles. |
|---|---|---|---|
| To New York | 278 | To North Elba | 30 |
| Elizabethtown | 8 | Lake Placid | 34 |
| Keene Flats (Head) | 24 | Saranac Lake | 42 |
| Keene | 20 | PAUL SMITH'S | 59 |

### No. 10.
#### ROOT'S

| To Elizabethtown | 23 | To Keene Flats | 25 |
|---|---|---|---|
| Crown Point | 22 | Boreas River | 13 |
| Schroon Lake | 9½ | Tahawas | 23 |
| Mud Pond | 10 | Halfway House | 31 |
| Upper Ausable | 16 | LONG LAKE | 45 |
| Top of Marcy | 21 | | |

### Route No. 11.
#### GLENS FALLS

| To New York | 204 | To Pottersville | 33 |
|---|---|---|---|
| Saratoga | 22 | Schroon | 42 |
| Lake George | 9 | Minerva | 41 |
| Warrensburgh | 15 | Newcomb | 63 |
| Chestertown | 27 | LONG LAKE | 77 |

### Route No. 12.
#### SARATOGA

| To New York | 182 | To Chestertown | 55 |
|---|---|---|---|
| Hadley (Luzerne) | 22 | Pottersville | 56 |
| Thurman | 36 | SCHROON | 65 |
| The Glen | 44 | ROOT'S | 74 |
| Riverside | 50 | | |

### Route No. 13.
#### FULTON CHAIN OF LAKES.

The usual gate of entrance from the south-west is made by leaving the Black River Railroad at Boonville or Port Leyden, thence by wagon to Arnolds, 23 miles; 2½ miles further is the foot of first lake; the first three are closely connected, and collectively, about 4 miles in length; the fourth lake is the largest, 6 miles long, and contains a number of pretty islands, the fifth and sixth mere ponds — between them a portage of three-quarters of a mile; from sixth to seventh 1½ miles by stream, seventh to eighth ½ mile by stream and ½ mile carry; seventh and eighth are each about 2 miles long; then another 1½ mile carry to the inlet and 4 miles by stream; 30 miles in all from Arnold's to the Raquette.

## Route No. 14.

### BARTLETT'S

| | Miles. |
|---|---|
| To Daniels | 2 |
| By Portage ($1.50) | 5 |
| Down Raquette River to Tupper's Lake | 16 |
| To Carey's | 2 |
| By Carry (75 cts.) | 3 |
| By Boat through Stony Creek Ponds | 5 |

| | Miles. |
|---|---|
| To Raquette River | 8 |
| To Mother Johnson's | 15 |
| By Portage ($1.50) | 16½ |
| To Cold River | 21½ |
| To Long Lake | 22½ |
| To Island House | 23 |
| To KELLOGG'S | 32 |

## No. 15.

### TUPPER'S LAKE.

#### MARTIN MOODY'S

| To Head of Lake | 6 |
| Setting-pole Rapids | 6 |
| Big Wolf Pond | 5 |
| Daniel's Carry | 11 |

| To Bartlett's | 16 |
| Little Tupper's | 15 |
| Lake Pleasant | 6 |
| MUD LAKE | 22 |

## Route No. 16.

### LONG LAKE TO TUPPER'S LAKE.

#### KELLOGG'S

| To Island House | 9 | 9 |
| To Outlet | ½ | |
| Through River | 6 | 15½ |
| Carry to Johnson's | 1½ | 16½ |
| To TUPPER'S LAKE | 28 | 44½ |
| To Head of Lake | 7 | 51½ |
| By boat and carry to little Tupper's Lake | 6 | 57½ |

| Little Tupper's | 3½ | 61 |
| Through Creek, Pond and Carry (one of 3 miles), to Long Lake, via Slim and Clear Ponds | 15 | 76 |

ROUTES. 159

### Route No. 17.
### LONG LAKE TO BLUE MOUNTAIN LAKE,
and return via South Pond.
#### KELLOGG'S

|  | Miles. |  |  |  | Miles. |
|---|---|---|---|---|---|
| To head of Lake.... | 3½ | 3½ | By River........... | ¼ | 26¾ |
| By River........... | ½ | 4 | Through Utowana L. | 2½ | 29¼ |
| By Carry........... | ½ | 4½ | By Stream to Eagle L. | ¾ | 30 |
| To Buttermilk Falls. | ¾ | 5¼ | To "Eagle's Nest".. | ¾ | 30¾ |
| By Carry........... | ¼ | 5½ | To BLUE MT. LAKE. | ½ | 31¼ |
| By River........... | 1½ | 7 | Across Lake....... | 2½ | 33¾ |
| By Portage......... | 1½ | 8½ | By Carry to South |  |  |
| Through Forked L., | 4 | 12½ | Pond............ | 3 | 36¾ |
| By Helmes Carry to |  |  | By Boat............ | 1½ | 38¼ |
| RAQUETTE LAKE. | ½ | 13 | By Carry to L. Lake. | 1 | 39¼ |
| To mouth Marion R. | 7 | 20 | To KELLOGG'S Ho- |  |  |
| By River........... | 6 | 26 | TEL............. | 3 | 42½ |
| By Carry.......... | ½ | 26½ |  |  |  |

### Route No. 18.
### NEWCOMB TO LONG LAKE.

From "Aunt Polly's" by boat through Belden Pond; carry of 12 rods; Rich Lake, 3½ miles; W. branch of river, 1 mile; Catlin Lake stream to Lillypad Pond, then Long Pond, 1 mile; Catlin Lake, 3½ miles; Round Pond 1 mile; 1½ mile carry to shore of Long Lake; Island House, ½ mile; a little over 12 miles in all.

### No. 19.
### JOHN DAVIS'

| To Kellogg's............ | 14 | To Tahawas ............ | 8 |
| Mt. Joseph............ | 6 | Adirondack .......... | 18 |
| North Creek......... | 30 | GLENS FALLS ........ | 63 |
| Pottersville .......... | 30 |  |  |

### No. 20.
### ADIRONDACK VILLAGE

| To Lower Works....... | 10 | To Avalanche Lake. ... | 7½ |
| Mud Pond .......... | 18 | Lake Harkness ..... | 1 |
| Indian Pass......... | 6 | Lake Andrews ...... | 2 |
| North Elba ......... | 16 | Preston Ponds...... | 3 |
| Calamity Pond...... | 4 | MARCY, Top ........ | 12 |
| Lake Colden........ | 6 |  |  |

## No. 21.
### KEENE FLATS.
#### DIBBLE'S

| | Miles. | | Miles. |
|---|---|---|---|
| To Keene | 5 | To Giant, Top | 6 |
| Elizabethtown | 13 | Marcy, Top, via John's Brook | 9 |
| Westport | 21 | | |
| Keeseville | 31 | Roaring Brook Falls | 3 |
| Plattsburgh | 39 | Chapel Pond | 4 |
| Lake Placid | 19 | Mud Pond | 17 |
| Saranac Lake | 28 | Root's | 27 |

### Route No. 22.
### ROUND TRIP.
#### DIBBLE'S

| | | | |
|---|---|---|---|
| To Widow Beede's | 2½ | To John Brown's Grave | 43 |
| Lower Ausable | 6 | Lake Placid | 46 |
| Upper Ausable | 9 | Top of Whiteface | 53 |
| Marcy, Top | 14 | Mountain House | 59 |
| Lake Colden | 20 | Wilmington Notch | 65 |
| Calamity Pond | 22 | North Elba | 71 |
| Iron Works | 27 | Keene | 82 |
| Indian Pass | 33 | BACK TO DIBBLE'S | 87 |
| Blinn's | 43 | | |

### No. 23.
#### BOSTON

| | | | |
|---|---|---|---|
| To Bellows Falls | 114 | To Quebec | 420 |
| White R. Junc | 154 | Troy | 240 |
| Rutland | 166 | Utica | 330 |
| Burlington | 234 | Syracuse | 383 |
| St. Albans | 267 | Rochester | 485 |
| Rouse's Point | 289 | Buffalo | 532 |
| Chateaugay | 336 | Niagara Falls | 541 |
| Ogdensburg | 409 | CHICAGO | 972 |
| Montreal | 337 | | |

### No. 24.
#### MONTREAL

| | | | |
|---|---|---|---|
| To Quebec | 180 | To Toronto | 333 |
| White Mountains | 201 | Hamilton | 372 |
| Portland | 292 | Niagara Falls | 400 |
| New York | 403 | Detroit | 547 |
| Boston | 337 | Chicago | 831 |
| Saratoga | 212 | ST. LOUIS | 1126 |
| Ottawa | 167 | | |

ROUTES. 161

## FARES TO DIFFERENT POINTS.

| | |
|---|---|
| New York to Albany — H. R. R. R................ | $3 60 |
| New York to Albany — Day and night boats....... | 2 00 |
| Albany to Binghamton — Albany & Susquehanna R. R. | 4 25 |
| Albany to Saratoga — R. & S. R. R ................ | 1 20 |
| Albany to Glens Falls............................. | 1 95 |
| Albany to Champlain Steamers.................... | 2 60 |
| Albany to Rutland............................ ..... | 3 20 |
| Albany to Lake George via Glens Falls ............ | 3 20 |
| Albany to Ticonderoga via Lake Champlain steamers, | 3 60 |
| Albany to Westport............................... | 4 60 |
| Albany to Port Kent........................... ... | 5 70 |
| Albany to Plattsburgh ............................ | 6 20 |
| Albany to Plattsburgh via Lake George............ | 9 20 |
| Albany to Rouse's Point...................  ...... | 6 60 |
| Albany to Montreal via Bur. & Vt. Central R. R..... | 8 60 |
| Albany to Montreal via Lake George .. ............ | 11 45 |
| Lake George Steamers (Excursion).................. | 2 00 |
| Whitehall to Rouse's Point (Champlain steamers).... | 4 00 |
| Saratoga to Profile House, via Lake Champlain,.... | 10 45 |
| Saratoga to Profile House, via Lakes George and Champlain ........................................ | 14 35 |
| Saratoga to Crawford House, via Lake Champlain.. | 11 20 |
| Saratoga to Newport, via Lake Champlain ......... | 9 45 |
| Saratoga to Burlington, via Lakes George and Champlain ............................................ | 7 25 |
| Saratoga to Plattsburgh, via Lakes George and Champlain .. ...................... ................. | 8 00 |
| Saratoga to Montreal, via Lakes George and Champlain............................... ............. | 10 25 |
| Saratoga to Montreal, via Lakes George and Champlain, Ogdensburg and the St. Lawrence........... | 16 00 |
| Excursion from Saratoga, through Lake George to Ticonderoga, and return by Champlain steamers, stopping over night at Caldwell ................... | 7 00 |

## To the Hunting Grounds.

| | |
|---|---|
| NEW YORK to Albany, via H. R. R. R.; Whitehall, via Rensselaer and Saratoga R. R.; Champlain steamers to Plattsburgh, rail to Point of Rocks, and stage to Paul Smith's or Martin's, (about) | $15 00 |
| NEW YORK to Port Kent, as above; then via Keeseville and Point of Rocks to Martin's or Paul Smith's by stage, | 13 50 |
| NEW YORK to Elizabethtown, via same route to Westport, then 8 miles of staging | 9 20 |
| ELIZABETHTOWN to Keene (12 miles by stage) | 1 50 |
| ELIZABETHTOWN to North Elba (Lake Placid), stage | 2 00 |
| ELIZABETHTOWN to Martin's (34 miles by stage) | 3 00 |
| NEW YORK to SCHROON LAKE, via Albany, Saratoga and Adirondack Railroad to Riverside; thence by stage to Pottersville, six miles, and by Steamer Effingham to Schroon, nine miles | 9 75 |
| NEW YORK to LONG LAKE, via Albany, Saratoga and Adirondack Railroad, to North Creek, fifty-seven miles, and stage via Minerva and Newcomb to C. H. Kellogg's (about) | 13 00 |
| FROM BOSTON, via Fitchburgh, Bellows Falls, Rutland, Burlington, Plattsburgh and Point of Rocks, to Paul Smith's or Martin's and return by same route, | 22 00 |

The fashionable round trip in connection with this is from Martin's to Paul Smith's, via Saranac Lakes and others by boat, or the same passed in reverse order. See Route No. 8.

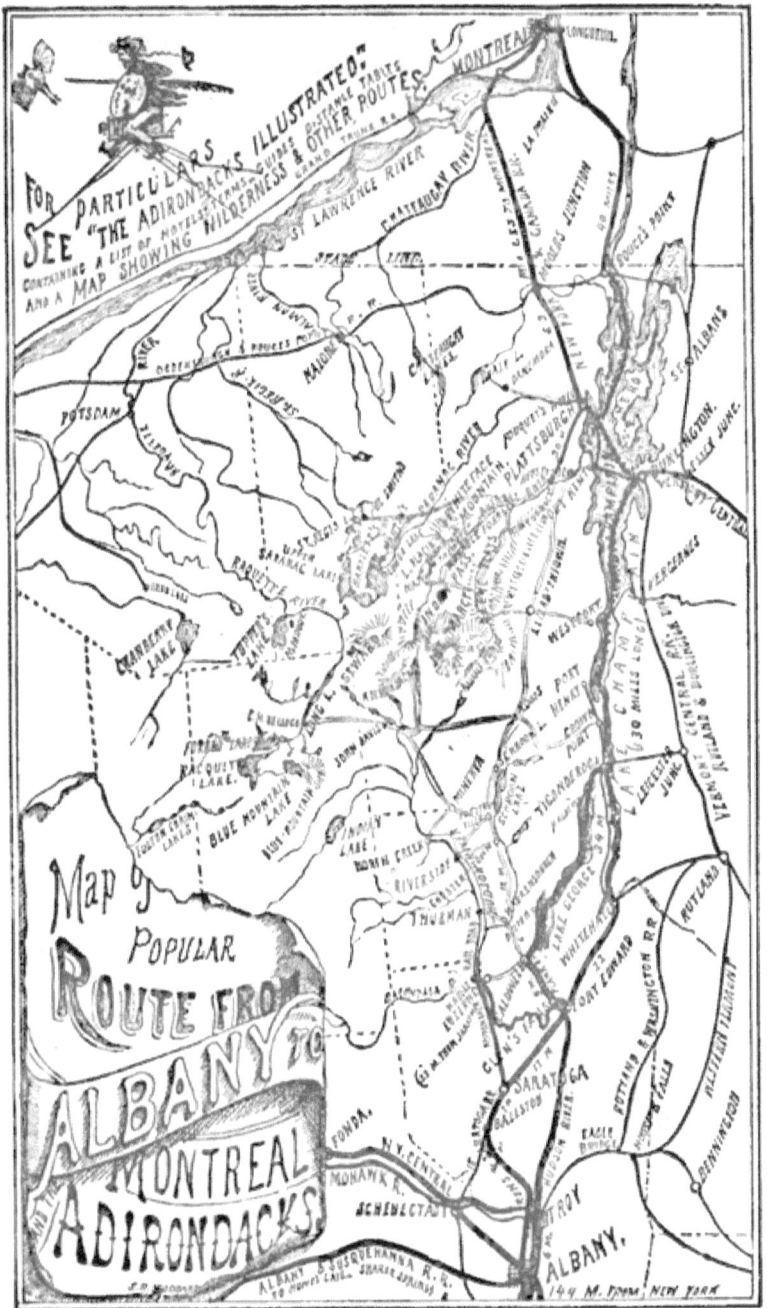

## DELAWARE & HUDSON CANAL CO.

THREE passenger trains each way, daily, over the Rensselaer & Saratoga R. R., connecting at GLENS FALLS with stages for LAKE GEORGE, at WHITEHALL with LAKE CHAMPLAIN STEAMERS, and at RUTLAND with Vermont Central R. R. for the north and east.

During the season of pleasure travel, FAST THROUGH EXPRESS TRAINS are run between New York, Saratoga and Glens Falls, for Lake George, Saratoga, Sharon Springs and Philadelphia via Wilkesbarre, Pa., connecting at Binghamton with trains on the Erie Railway, for the west and south-west.

Connection is made at Albany and Troy with Day and Night lines of Steamers on the Hudson.

### TRAINS NORTH.

| STATIONS. | 1 A.M. | 81 A.M. | 3 P.M. | 5 P.M. | 7 P.M. | 9 P.M. | 11 P.M. |
|---|---|---|---|---|---|---|---|
| Albany .......... Le. | .... | *7.00 | *1.15 | *4.30 | .... | .... | 7.15 |
| Troy .............. | *7.15 | .... | *1.45 | *4.50 | 1.25 | 8.20 | .... |
| Round Lake ...... | *8.12 | *7.57 | 2.35 | *5.47 | .... | .... | 8.26 |
| Ballston .......... | 8.28 | 8.12 | 2.53 | 6.05 | .... | .. | 8.37 |
| Saratoga ......... | 9.00 | 8.30 | 3.20 | 6.35 | 2.25 | 9.20 | 8.50 |
| Fort Edward ...... | 9.42 | .... | 4.02 | 7.15 | .... | .... | .... |
| Glens Falls ..... Ar. | 10.10 | .... | 4.30 | 7.40 | .... | .... | .... |
| Glens Falls .... Le. | 8.40 | .... | 3.15 | 6.40 | .... | .... | .... |
| Whitehall ..... Ar. | 10.35 | .... | 4.55 | 8.05 | ... | .... | .... |
| Lake ............... | 10.45 | .... | ... | 8.20 | .... | .... | .... |
| Rutland ........ Ar. | 11.50 | .... | .... | 9.05 | ... | .... | 8.55 |

### TRAINS SOUTH.

| STATIONS. | 2 A.M. | 4 A.M. | 6 P.M. | 88 P.M. | 8 A.M. | 10 P.M. | 32 A.M. |
|---|---|---|---|---|---|---|---|
| Rutland.. ...... Le. | 5.00 | 8.30 | 4.00 | .... | .... | .... | 10.00 |
| Lake ............... | 5.50 | .... | 4.45 | .... | .... | .... | .... |
| Whitehall ......... | 6.10 | 10.35 | 5.05 | .... | .... | .... | .... |
| Glens Falls .. Ar. | 7.30 | 12.30 | 6.30 | .... | .... | .... | .... |
| Glens Falls ... Le. | 6.40 | 11.10 | 5.40 | .... | .... | .. . | .... |
| Fort Edward...... | 7.04 | 11.28 | 5.56 | . .. | .... | .... | 12.00 |
| Saratoga ......... | 7.55 | 12.15 | 6.45 | 6.55 | 9.10 | 4.00 | 6.30 |
| Ballston .......... | 8.12 | 12.33 | 7.04 | 7.11 | .... | .... | 6.45 |
| Round Lake.... Le. | *8.28 | 12.50 | *7.21 | *7.26 | .... | .... | 6.56 |
| Troy .......... Ar. | 9.25 | 1.40 | 8.15 | .. | 10.10 | 5.00 | .... |
| Albany .......... Ar. | 9.50 | 2.00 | .... | 8.30 | .... | .... | 8.15 |

\* Trains Nos. 1, 81, 3 and 5 for Saratoga, Fort Edward and Whitehall, connect at Glens Falls for Lake George. Nos. 1 and 5 connect at Whitehall with Steamers on Lake Champlain for all points north, and at Rutland with Trains for north and east. No. 11 connects *from* Day Boat for Saratoga.

† Nos. 2 and 4 connect with Express Trains for New York. No. 6 connects at Troy with Citizens' Line Steamers. No. 88 at Albany with People's Line Steamers for New York. No. 12 at Albany with Day Line Steamer.

For rates of fare, tickets or information, apply to ticket agents of any connecting line, or to the undersigned.

H. V. OLYPHANT,      S. E. MAYO,
Ass't Pres't, Albany, N. Y.      Gen. Ticket Agt.

# CONDENSED TIME TABLE
### BETWEEN
# NEW YORK AND MONTREAL,
### VIA
## Lake Champlain and Saratoga.

VERMONT, Capt. Wm. H. Flagg.
CHAMPLAIN, Capt. Geo. Rushlow.
ADIRONDACK, Capt. Wm. Anderson.
A. WILLIAMS, Capt. B. J. Holt.

Forming two lines daily each way (Sundays excepted), between Whitehall and Rouse's Point. The Steamers comprising the line are entirely new, and are, as they always have been, models of neatness and comfort. Their general arrangements, decoration and finish are of the most artistic and luxurious character, and every attention is guaranteed the passenger.

| GOING SOUTH. | | | GOING NORTH. | | |
|---|---|---|---|---|---|
| STATIONS. | Night Boat on Lake. | Day Boat on Lake. | STATIONS. | Night Boat on Lake. | Day Boat on Lake. |
| Lv. Montreal | 3.15 p m | 6.10 a m | Lv. N.Y., via H.R.R.R. | 10.45 a m | 11.00 p m |
| " Rouse's Point | 5.55 " | 8. 0 " | " " " Steamboat | ...... | 6.00 " |
| " Plattsburgh | 7.30 " | 8.00 " | " Albany | 4.30 p m | 7.00 a m |
| " Port Kent | 8.40 " | 9.00 " | " Troy | 4.50 " | 7.15 " |
| " Burlington | 9.30 " | 10.45 " | " Schenectady | 5.00 " | 7.23 " |
| " Ticonderoga | 3.30 a m | 2.3 p m | " Saratoga | 6.45 " | 9.40 " |
| Ar. Caldwell | ...... | 7.00 " | " Whitehall | 8.30 " | 10.50 " |
| " Whitehall | 5.30 a m | 4.45 " | " Caldwell | ...... | 7.45 " |
| " Saratoga | 7.40 " | 6.35 " | Ar. Ticonderoga | 10.30 " | 12.50 p m |
| " Troy | 9.25 " | 8.15 " | " Burlington | 3.00 a m | 5.00 " |
| " Albany | 9.50 " | 8.30 " | " Port Kent | 3.40 " | 5.35 " |
| " Schenectady | 9.15 " | 7.55 " | " Plattsburgh | 5.00 " | 6.30 " |
| " N. Y., via Steamboat | ...... | 6.00 a m | " Rouse's Point | 7.15 " | 8.30 " |
| " " H.R.R.R. | 3.30 p m | 6.00 " | " Montreal | 10.05 " | 10.30 " |
| | | | " Ogdensburg | 12.35 p m | ...... |

### CONNECTIONS.

AT WHITEHALL, with trains of Rensselaer & Saratoga R. R., for Saratoga, Troy, Albany, New York, and all Southern and Western points.
AT TICONDEROGA, with Steamer Minnehaha through Lake George.
AT BURLINGTON, with trains of Rutland & Burlington and Central Vermont Railroads, for all Southern and Eastern points, and the mountains of Vermont and New Hampshire.
AT PORT KENT, with stages for Keeseville and the Adirondack Sporting Region.
AT PLATTSBURGH, with trains of N. Y. & C. R. R. for the Hunting and Fishing localities o' the Saranac Lakes and the Adirondack Wilderness.
AT ROUSE'S POINT, with trains of O. & L. C. and Grand Trunk Railways for Ogdensburg, Montreal, Quebec, and all points in Northern New York and Canada.

Trains leave PLATTSBURGH FOR AUSABLE STATION at 7.30 A. M. and 3.00 P. M. Returning arrive at Plattsburgh at 11.15 A. M. and 6 P. M.
Daily line of four-horse Coaches leave Ausable for the forest resorts on arrival of morning mail. A. L. INMAN, *Gen'l Supt.*

## VERMONT CENTRAL.

**T**HE VERMONT CENTRAL RAILROAD passes through the loveliest scenery of the old Granite State, up the valley of the Connecticut, and through the Green Mountains, breaking through the western barrier between Mansfield and Camel's Hump to Essex Junction, Burlington, St. Albans, thence north and west, making one of the nearest, grandest, and most direct route from the south and east to the Adirondacks, Montreal, the Thousand Islands and the Great West. Drawing room cars by day and sleeping cars by night; easy riding; luxuriously furnished, well ventilated coaches; sure connections, and quick time guaranteed to patrons of the road.

J. W. HOBART,      J. GREGORY SMITH,
*Gen. Sup't.*      *President.*

### TIME TABLE.

| [Read down.] Trains leave. | | | | | | [Read up.] Trains arrive. | | |
|---|---|---|---|---|---|---|---|---|
| Exp. P.M. | Pass. A.M. | Exp. P.M. | Miles. | STATIONS. | Miles. | Exp. P.M. | Exp. P.M. | Mail. P.M. |
| 3.00 | 8.05 | 8.10 | | ....New York.... | 425 | .... | 12.35 | 11.12 |
| | | | | | | | A.M. | P.M. |
| 5.50 | 11.00 | 11.20 | | ...New Haven... | | .... | 9.41 | 8.30 |
| P.M. | .M. | A.M. | | | | P.M. | A.M. | P.M. |
| 3.17 | 8.10 | 5.00 | | ...New London... | | .... | 11.15 | 9.32 |
| 5½.0 | 11.10 | 7½.8 | .. | ......Boston...... | ... | 10.20 | 8.35 | 6.23 |
| P.M. | P.M. | A.M. | | | | | | |
| 10.00 | 4.30 | 10.07 | 0 | ..South Vernon... | 237 | ... | 4.47 | 3.55 |
| 10.20 | 4.55 | 10.30 | 10 | ..Brattleboro'... | 227 | 9.40 | 4.20 | 3.30 |
| 11.15 | 5.55 | 11.32 | 34 | ..Bellows Falls... | 203 | 7.40 | 3.25 | 2.10 |
| 12.20 | 7.20 | 12.45 | 60 | .....Windsor..... | 177 | 5.52 | 2.10 | 1.20 |
| A.M. | A.M. | P.M. | | | | | | |
| 1.00 | 4.50 | 1.30 | 74 | White River Junc. | 163 | 4.55 | 1.20 | 11.55 |
| 3.20 | 7.25 | 3.30 | 127 | ....Northfield..... | 110 | 2.56 | 10.36 | 9.30 |
| 3.50 | 7.45 | 3.40 | 138 | ....Montpelier.... | 101 | 2.40 | 10.20 | 9.15 |
| 4.42 | 9.05 | 4.55 | 176 | ....Burlington.... | 75 | 1.40 | 9.00 | 8.00 |
| 6.10 | 10.45 | 6.15 | 195 | ....St. Albans.... | 42 | 12.15 | 7.25 | 6.20 |
| 9.10 | .... | 9.10 | 259 | .....Montreal..... | ... | 9.15 | 3.45 | .... |
| A.M. | P.M. | P.M. | | | | A.M. | P.M. | A.M. |
| 6.30 | 12.10 | 6.35 | 195 | ...St. Albans. | 141 | 11.55 | 7.05 | 5.55 |
| 7.40 | 1.18 | 7.40 | 218 | ..Rouse's Point.. | 118 | 10.53 | 5.55 | 3.57 |
| 10.05 | 5.15 | 10.25 | 275 | .....Malone..... | 61 | 8.35 | 3.10 | 10.25 |
| 12.30 | 8.00 | 12.40 | 336 | ...Ogdensburg... | 0 | 6.00 | 12.35 | 6.00 |

### RUTLAND DIVISION.

| P.M. | P.M. | A.M. | | | | P.M. | A.M. | P.M. |
|---|---|---|---|---|---|---|---|---|
| 6.30 | 11.15 | 11.50 | 0 | ..Bellows Falls.. | 120 | 2.20 | 3.20 | .... |
| 11.00 | 1.40 | 2.00 | 53 | ....Rutland. .. | 67 | 11.40 | 12.32 | 7.00 |
| | | | | | | P.M. | | |
| .... | 3.15 | 3.30 | 86 | ...Middlebury... | 34 | 9.45 | 10.58 | 5.01 |
| .... | 4.40 | 4.55 | 120 | ...Burlington... | 0 | 7.55 | 9.10 | 2.00 |
| .... | 9.10 | 9.10 | 216 | ....Montreal..... | .... | .... | 3.45 | .... |

## FOUQUET'S HOTEL

IS situated at Plattsburgh, N. Y., upon the banks of Cumberland Bay, near the scene of the naval battle of 1814. Its Piazzas afford delightful views of the Lake, the Islands, the Green Mountains on the east, and the Adirondacks on the south. It has a retired situation, pleasure, and flower grounds, fount of spring-water, spacious and well ventilated rooms, which, together with the pleasant drives in the vicinity, offer attractions to the seeker after health and pleasure, that cannot be surpassed.

It has ever been noted as the principal resting place for parties en route between Montreal and Lake George, and from it via railway from Plattsburgh to Point of Rocks, the most interesting parts of the great Adirondacks can be reached with more convenience and dispatch than from any other point.

During the past winter this hotel has been completely renovated and put in the most elegant condition for the accommodation of guests. Transient guests charged as heretofore.

Maps, Guides to the great wilderness and a complete line of Stoddard's "Crystal" views of Ausable Chasm at the office.

For particulars and further information address

L. M. FOUQUET, Plattsburgh, N. Y.

### AUSABLE HOUSE.
#### KEESEVILLE, N. Y.

The Ausable House, located in the midst of a wild, picturesque and romantic country, is a desirable resort for season boarders. Rooms large; will accommodate 100. Terms, $3 per day, transient; per week, $9 to $14.

E. AVERILL, Proprietor.

ROUTE. — Nearest and best route to the Saranacs, St. Regis and the Adirondacks, is via Lake Champlain steamers to Port Kent; thence by Coaches to Keeseville; by Stages or Livery from Keeseville to destination. 40 minutes from Port Kent; 30 minutes to Ausable Chasm; 4 hours to Whiteface Mountain, and 9 hours to the sporting grounds of the Saranacs and St. Regis — most of the route by Plank Road, through a picturesque and beautiful country.

### HARPER & TUFTS.

HARPER & TUFT'S line of easy-riding four-horse coaches run to the Adirondack hunting and fishing grounds daily, meeting the Champlain steamers at Port Kent, running thence to Keeseville, up the lovely valley of the Ausable to Martin's and Paul Smith's at the Saranac and St. Regis Lakes, or to Martin's via Whiteface Mountain, Wilmington Pass, John Brown's Grave, Lake Placid, etc.

Private carriages will be furnished to meet parties at Port Kent, etc., or for excursions when required.

Address    HARPER & TUFTS, Keeseville, N. Y.

## AUSABLE CHASM.

THE CHASM HOUSE is a large, pleasantly situated stone building, overlooking Birmingham Falls, at the head of Ausable Chasm, 1½ miles from Keeseville and 3 from Port Kent, affording a delightful retreat with hotel fare and country quiet. The rooms are large and airy, affording accommodation for 25. Terms $7 per week. Address H. H. Bromley, Keeseville, N. Y.

## ST. REGIS LAKE.

PAUL SMITH'S St. Regis House needs no comment. It is situated on the lower St. Regis lake, 38 miles from Ausable station, 14 miles from Martin's; has accommodations for 100 guests; is first-class in every respect, and patronized by the very best class of people in the country. Daily stages to R. R. Telegraph in the House. Boats, guides and camp supplies furnished. Terms $2.50 per day. Address A. A. Smith, Bloomingdale, Essex county.

## SARANAC LAKE.

MARTIN'S, at the Lower Saranac, is the largest Hotel in the Adirondacks, at the regular entrance to the Lake region; is a first-class House, containing large rooms, nicely furnished; double piazza; long, pleasant parlor fronting the lake. Telegraph in the House. Daily line of stage to Ausable station, 36 miles distant. Boats, guides and supplies furnished; will accommodate 200. Terms $2.50 per day, $14 per week. Address Wm. F. Martin, Saranac Lake, Essex county.

## UPPER SARANAC.

BARTLETT'S is at the foot of the Carry, between Round Lake and the Upper Saranac, 12 miles from Martin's, on the fashionable round trip to Paul Smith's and the Long and Tupper's lakes route — a popular hunting and fishing resort — where every thing necessary for the sport can be obtained at a reasonable price. Will accommodate 50 guests. For further information address V. C. Bartlett, Saranac Lake, Essex county, N. Y.

## NASH'S.

NASH'S, on the west shore of Mirror Lake, facing the Great Peaks of the Adirondacks, within 80 rods of Lake Placid, is open from June to November, with accommodations for 25 guests. Terms, $2 per day, $7 per week. From Ausable Station, 26 miles distant, the road passes by the base of Whiteface Mountain, the natural flume, Big Falls, and through grand old Wilmington pass. A picturesque drive of 28 miles leads to Elizabethtown.

Private conveyances, boats and guides furnished at reasonable rates when desired. (See page 75.)

Address       J. V. NASH,
       North Elba, Essex Co., N. Y.

## LAKE PLACID HOUSE.

THE LAKE PLACID HOUSE, B. F. Brewster, proprietor, is situated on Lake Placid; is new; rooms large and plainly furnished; will accommodate 60 guests. Terms, from $8 to $10 per week.

Boats, camping necessaries, etc., to let, with or without guides.

Address     B. F. BREWSTER,
       North Elba, Essex Co., N. Y.

## LYON'S HOTEL,
### NORTH ELBA, N. Y.,

IS situated on the post-road between *Elizabethtown* and *Saranac Lake*, two miles from Lake Placid and one and a half miles from John Brown's grave. Excellent river and brook fishing near by. Post-office in the house; teams in readiness to convey guests to any place required; will accommodate 25. Terms, $1.50 per day, $8 per week. Address    M. C. LYON,
       North Elba, Essex Co., N. Y.

## NEWCOMB.

THE HALF-WAY HOUSE, John Davis, proprietor, is on the regular route to Long Lake, 14 miles distant and 30 miles from Pottersville and the Adirondack R. R. at North Creek. Stages leave *North Creek* daily stopping over night at Olmsteadville, leave Olmsteadville for Long Lake on Wednesday and Saturday mornings at 6 o'clock. Returning leave Long Lake on Tuesday and Friday mornings at 7, stopping each way for dinner, at the Half-way House.

Guests desiring to stop over will find comfortable quarters and a table supplied with the best the forest affords. Those wishing to take *the* NEW WATER ROUTE TO LONG LAKE, will here find Guides, Boats and all supplies necessary *for camping purposes* — will accommodate 20 guests. Terms per day $2.00, per week $10.00; 4 mails weekly. Address John Davis, Newcomb, Essex Co., N. Y.

## WHITEFACE MOUNTAIN.

WHITEFACE MOUNTAIN HOUSE, S. H. Weston, proprietor, is situated at the eastern base of "Old Whiteface. It is 13 miles from Ausable station, 12 from North Elba, 3 from the Natural Flume, 4 from Big Falls, 6 from Wilmington Notch and 6 from the summit of Whiteface Mountain. Horses, carriages and guides in readiness for excursions or the ascent of Whiteface, will take care of 50. Terms $2.00 per day, $9 per week. Address T. J. Baldwin, agent, Wilmington, N. Y.

## TUPPER'S LAKE.

MARTIN MOODY, situated at the foot of Big Tupper Lake in the midst of the best hunting and fishing ground in the wilderness, is prepared to furnish boats, guides and supplies to sportsmen throughout the season. The House will accommodate 50 guests. Terms, $1.50 per day, $10.00 per week. Address Martin Moody, Saranac Lake, Franklin Co., N. Y.

See pages 91, 92 and 158.

## LONG LAKE HOTEL.

LONG LAKE is one of the loveliest sheets of water in that magnificent region of lakes and streams, stretching through the wilderness in a northeasterly direction for 14 miles, an ever-changing panorama of bay and headland, from the rapids at its head to the beautiful natural meadow at its outlet; it is but little more than a mile at the widest and contains several pretty islands, Round Island near its center being a perfect little gem. Fishing is excellent here, the lake containing, besides its trout and other fish common to Adirondack waters, an immense number of pickerel, making rare sport for those inclined to troll. Away toward the north and east are the great mountain peaks, on the west a mass of streams and ponds that afford fine fishing and hunting, while to the south are the noted Raquette waters, making it what it is often called, a sportsman's paradise indeed. Three miles from its head is the little village of Long Lake, noted for the manufacture of Adirondack boats and as being the home of some of the best guides that the wilderness has ever produced.

THE LONG LAKE HOTEL, without which the region would lose a great deal of its attraction to the sportsman, is a few rods from the lake shore, a large roomy house that can take care of 30 comfortably; the table is seldom without its trout or venison during the season and terms very reasonable for such fare ($10 per week). Stages leave and arrive twice each week, running to North Creek and Pottersville, 44 miles distant, boats and camp equipages furnished, and guides engaged when desired (guides are here all "independent"). For particulars address C. H. Kellogg, Long Lake, Hamilton Co., remembering that it takes two or three days for a letter to reach that wild region. For distance tables, etc., see "Routes."

## MANSION HOUSE.

### SIMONDS & KELLOGG, Proprietors.

THIS popular hotel is situated in the pleasant little village of Elizabethtown, among the outskirts of the Adirondacks, in the beautiful valley of the Boquet, near the junction of the Little Boquet, the view it commands is unrivaled. Is located on high ground which makes it particularly favorable for the entertainment of summer residents during the season, and can accommodate 200 guests. Our four-horse coach runs to the Lake Champlain steamboat landing, at Westport, eight miles, twice a day. Good horses and carriages can at all times be had for the accommodation of guests, and at reasonable rates. Terms, $10 per week. Address as above.

### DISTANCE FROM MANSION HOUSE

| | |
|---|---|
| To Westport (steamboat landing) | 8 miles. |
| " Port Henry | 18 " |
| " Keene | 11 " |
| " Head Keene Flats | 16 " |
| " To Ausable Ponds | 20 " |
| " North Elba (John Brown's grave) | 22 " |
| " Lake Placid | 25 " |
| " Saranac Lakes | 33 " |
| " Paul Smith's | 40 " |
| " Lewis | 4 " |
| " Keeseville | 22 " |
| " New Russia | 4 " |
| " Split Rock Falls | 8 " |
| " New Pond | 10 " |
| " Root's Hotel (Schroon river) | 23 " |
| " Schroon Lake | 32 " |
| " Black Pond | 6 " |

The distance from Westport to Saranac Lakes via Elizabethtown, Keene and North Elba is 41 miles; the most direct, and, in every respect, the best and cheapest route. Stage fare, $3.

Good conveyance can always be found ready to take people to any part of the Adirondacks at very low rates.

## TAHAWUS HOUSE,

### KEENE FLATS.

THE TAHAWUS HOUSE is located on a level plateau a little above the river, within three miles of the head of Keene Flats, commanding a magnificent view of the grand mountains around — Old Hurricane, Spread Eagle, the Giant of the Valley, Mount Dix, Noon-mark and others, the grand mass of broken, rugged mountain ranges and peaks toward the south and west, and within an hour's drive and walk of twenty gorges, flumes, passes, and cascades, the wildest and most beautiful that can be found in the Adirondack region. Keene Flats has but very recently been brought before the public, hidden as it is among the highest of the mountains, and then it flashed out like the revelation of an unknown land — now, standing as at the head of popular resorts for the artist and the refined lover of nature; the fishing near by is good, and the Ausable ponds toward the south, and forests in that direction are specially noted for large number of deer. The Tahawus House is nearly new, two stories high, well furnished, surrounded on two sides by a pleasant two story piazza, and will take care of forty guests very comfortably; it is 19 miles from Westport, over a good country road; 5 from Keene, with daily mails through the season. Guides and camping necessaries furnished when desired; also carriages for the lovely drives north and south, or to meet parties at the Champlain steamers. Terms $8 to $10 per week. See Keene Flats "routes." For further particulars address

N. M. DIBBLE,
Keene Flats, Essex county, N. Y.

## ADIRONDACK SPRINGS.

THESE Springs are beautifully situated upon an eastern slope of the chain of Adirondacks, ½ mile from the shore of Lake Champlain, 4 miles from Westport village and the same from the wide-awake village of Port Henry; 3 miles from the Cheever ore mines, and 5 from the extensive mines at Mineville. They are but 2 hours ride from the ruins of old Crown Point.

At the west is Bald Peak over 2,000 feet above tide water. A wagon road leading within ½ mile of summit from which an extensive view is presented of the mining districts, the towering peaks of the Adirondacks lying to the west, and at the east the Green Mountain State with her many villages and streams dotting the plains to the Canadian border.

Testimonials in pamphlet form with an analysis of the mineral waters cheerfully sent on application. Good accommodations for a number can be engaged by addressing the proprietor,

G. W. SPENCER,
Westport, Essex Co., N. Y.

## MOOERS.

THE JUNCTION HOUSE at Mooers is at the junction of the Rouse's Point & Ogdensburg and New York & Canada Railroads, in the direct line of travel from the north-west and Montreal to Plattsburgh, the principal gateway and easiest route to the Great Wilderness, and noted as the place "where in an unpretentious little house can be procured a dinner hardly surpassed by any hotel in the country," every attention is paid to the convenience of guests and in that great failing among hotels — want of cleanliness — the most fastidious can have no cause for complaint. Good hunting and fishing near by. Special attention given to commercial travelers. Horses and carriages furnished when desired, Terms $2.00 per day. Meals ready on the arrival of connecting trains. For further particulars address

HENRY W. LAWRENCE,
Mooers, N. Y.

## CRAWFORD HOUSE,
### KEENE FLATS, N. Y.

NEW house; new rooms; newly painted, papered and furnished—a table that the proprietor aims to make as good as any. A central position; daily mails, and the freedom of a home, with the accommodations of a hotel, are some of the attractions offered for 1874.

Teams furnished when desired; will accommodate twenty-five. Terms $7 per week.

Address        E. M. CRAWFORD,
Keene Flats, N. Y.

---

L. SMITH HOBART,     JOHN C. MOSS,     D. I. CARSON,
President.     Superintendent.     Gen'l Agent.

## PHOTO ENGRAVING CO.
### 62 Courtlandt St.
### NEW YORK.

Relief Plates for Newspaper, Book and Catalogue Illustrations Engraved in hard Type-Metal, by a new photographic process. Prints, Pen Drawings, Pencil Sketches and Photographs available. These plates are an excellent substitute for wood-cuts. *Their average cost is much less*, and they are preferable in other important respects. They can be printed perfectly on any ordinary press.

**TERMS CASH ON DELIVERY.**
*Send Stamp for Illustrated Circular.*

CONGRESS HALL, SARATOGA SPRINGS, N. Y.

11 x 14 PHOTOGRAPHS — $18 PER DOZ.

41. Black Mountain — matches with 42 and 43.
42. Tongue Mountain — matches with 41 and 43.
43. Point of the Tongue — matches with 41 and 42.
44. Lake George — Narrows from Sabbath Day Point.
45. Black Mountain from Sabbath Day Point.
46. Lake George — Black Mountain from the North.
47. Lake George — Looking South-west from Dresden.
48. Sabbath Day Point, Lake George.
49. Twin Mountains, Lake George.
50. The Beach, Sabbath Day Point, Lake George.
51. Lake George — View at Hague.
52. Roger's Rock, from Anthony's Nose, Lake George.
53. Roger's Slide, Lake George.
54. Ruins of Fort Ticonderoga — The Barracks.
55. Ruins of Fort Ticonderoga — Mount Defiance.
56. Ruins of Fort Ticonderoga — Tremble Meadow.
57. Steamer Adirondack.
58. Steamer Vermont.
59. Steamer Vermont, State-room Hall.
60. Ausable Chasm — Up the River from Table Rock.
61. Ausable Chasm — Up the River from Table Rock.
62. Ausable Chasm — The Boat Ride.
63. Ausable Chasm — Down from Table Rock.
64. Ausable Chasm — The Devil's Pulpit.
65. The Sentinel — Ausable Chasm.
66. Cathedral Rocks — Ausable Chasm.
67. Ausable Chasm — Down from the Punch Bowl.
68. Ausable Chasm — The Devil's Oven.
69. Birmingham Falls from Below.
70. Birmingham Falls from Above.
71. "The Walled Banks of the Ausable."
72. Poke-o-moonshine — Adirondack.
73. Rockwell's Hotel, Luzerne.
74. The Hudson at Luzerne — Up the River.
75. The Hudson at Luzerne — Down the River.
76. Luzerne Falls.
77. Luzerne Lake.
78. "The Wayside," Luzerne.
79. Sunlight and Shadow.

S. R. Stoddard, Photographer, Glen's Falls

STRONG'S REMEDIAL INSTITUTE.

RS. S. S. & S. E. STRONG'S REMEDIAL INSTITUTE, Saratoga Springs, N. Y., has Turkish, Russian, Sulphur-Air, Hydropathic, and Electro-Thermal Baths; Equalizer or Vacuum Treatment, Movement Cure, Laryngoscope, Inhalation, Oxygen Gas, Faradaic and Galvanic Electricity, Medicines, Health-lift, Gymnastics, for the treatment of Nervous, Lung, Female and Chronic Diseases.

For Description of Appliances, Diseases and their successful treatment, terms, etc., send for a Circular.

Its proprietors are Graduates of the Medical Department of the New York University. The Institution is the resort of leading men in Church and State for rest and recreation as well as treatment. The building is heated with steam and thoroughly ventilated, constituting it a most desirable Winter as well as a Summer Home.

Among our patrons are Rev. T. L. Cuyler, D. D., Brooklyn, Prof. Taylor Lewis, LL. D., Union College; Bishop E. S. Janes, D. D., New York City, etc.

## ROCKWELL'S HOTEL,

### LUZERNE, N. Y.

AMONG summer resorts easy of access, combining the advantages of first-class fare, lovely drives, boating, hunting and fishing, Luzerne has no peer in the country. It is situated on the Upper Hudson, just above its junction with the Sacandaga, 12 miles south-west of Lake George, and 22 miles north of Saratoga on the west side of the mountain that ends at the latter place.

Rockwell's Hotel, standing near the river side, has been for years a noted resort for the solid men of the country, and for sportsmen, as the junior Rockwell is one of the most successful hunters in the country, and thoroughly posted as to the sporting grounds of the great north woods.

The accommodations consist of the original hotel, containing the parlors, offices, sleeping apartments, the large dining room, one or two cottages and a pleasant roomy structure surrounded by a grand broad piazza, and separated by a little distance from the main building. It contains 30 large rooms finished off in suites for such as prefer their seclusion to that of the more public ones. The entire establishment is luxuriously furnished, the beds especially excellent, and the table unexcelled by the very best houses in the country.

It will accommodate 150. Terms, $3 per day; $14 to $17.50 per week, 2 trains daily to Saratoga; for further information apply to the proprietors,

Messrs. G. T. ROCKWELL & SON,
Luzerne, N. Y.

### ROCKWELL HOUSE.

THE ROCKWELL HOUSE is a new hotel, thoroughly furnished, large and well ventilated rooms; situate near the Falls of the Hudson and the Cave made classic by the pen of Cooper, within an hour's drive of Lake George, passing Williams' Monument, Bloody Pond, Old Fort Gage, and other historical points on the way. Reaching Glens Falls by the morning train, tourists have time for dinner, and an afternoon's drive to the lake. Arriving by the evening train they can secure a good night's rest, and a daylight ride to Lake George the next day.

Those intending to leave Lake George for the early morning train at Glens Falls will add to their pleasure by reaching the Rockwell House the evening before; thus securing a good night's rest, and a seasonable breakfast. Thus they will avoid rising at four o'clock in the morning, a ride of nine miles in a stage, and starting on a journey by railway without breakfast. Free omnibus to and from all trains.

Board, $3 per day; $14 to $21 per week.

ROCKWELL BROTHERS,
Glens Falls, N. Y.

## HALF-WAY HOUSE,

### French Mountain.

GEORGE BROWN'S half-way house is located between Glens Falls and Lake George, near the foot of French Mountain, and right on the battle-ground of the French and Indian War, where, in 1755, the Mohawk chief, King Hendrick, and Col. Ephraim Williams fell, the spot marked by a monument erected to the memory of the latter, who was the founder of Williams College.

WILLIAMS' MONUMENT.

This hotel is in fine condition, being newly furnished and painted, and for flowers, shrubbery, plants and shade has no superiors. The reception-room has the largest collection of Indian relics of the War of 1755-6 to be found in the country.

Trout and game suppers always served in season.

This hotel is well known by the traveling public as a first-class house for meals, and for the superior quality of its wines and liquors furnished by Mr. Brown, who has catered to the public taste at this place for the past twenty-eight years.

Address,   GEORGE BROWN,
French Mountain,
Warren Co., N. Y.

## FORT WILLIAM HENRY HOTEL.

LAKE GEORGE was re-discovered in 1868 by T. Roessle & Son, who raised, enlarged and reconstructed the old wigwam at its head to such an extent that its former friends could hardly recognize it in the elegant structure now known as the Fort William Henry Hotel. It is from four to six stories high, surmounted by a mansard roof, and has a lake frontage of three hundred and thirty-four feet. Along the entire front extends a piazza twenty-five feet wide, the roof supported by columns thirty feet in height. Above the center rises a dome flanked by two towers, while at the east end of the building is another nearly as high. The center is on one end just at present, but Mr. Roessle designs to even it up soon, and make it, when completed, one of the most imposing structures of the kind in the country, and be, in fact, what he delights to call it — a palace.

From the little balcony, hanging like a martin box high up on the dome, the tastefully arranged grounds may be seen spread out like a map beneath, while the beholder seems to have risen into a new world, with a widened vision which takes in over half the entire lake, extending away down into Northwest bay and over beyond the islands into the Narrows. Under the dome is the general office, which is also a point of general interest, made bright with the plumage of fair ladies; fresh and clean, with just a touch of color blending with its white and gold, and elegant in its rich simplicity.

## CENTRAL HOTEL,

(Nearly opposite the Lake House.)

LAKE GEORGE.

THIS house is pleasantly situated in the village of Caldwell, at the head of Lake George. It furnishes unsurpassed attractions to families, summer boarders, gentlemen of leisure and sportsmen. The table is supplied with choicest delicacies and substantials of the season, and the bar with the best of wines and liquors.

Good hunting and fishing. Woodcock, Partridge, Snipe, Deer, lake and brook Trout, Bass, Perch and Pickerel abound. Will accommodate 60. Terms $2.00 per day. Special rates by the week or season. Address,

B. O. BROWN,

Lake George, N. Y.

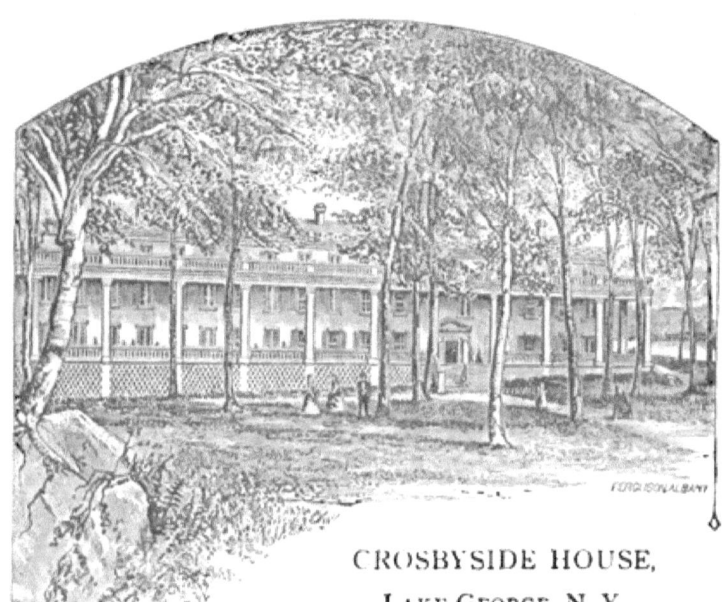

### CROSBYSIDE HOUSE,
#### LAKE GEORGE, N. Y.,

Is situated on the east shore of the lake, three-fourths of a mile from its head, formerly known as the United States Hotel. During the last year it has been enlarged and improved, and now has accommodations for 200 guests. Three cottages on the grounds belonging to the house; a dock where all Lake George steamers land; a fleet of small boats for the accommodation of guests; hourly ferry to Caldwell, carrying mails, etc. Situated on a breezy, tree-covered point, commanding one of the finest and most extended views on the lake, the very first class of society, and a table that we try to make as good as any found in the country are among the attractions at Crosbyside.

Terms $14 to $25 per week. Address,

F. G. CROSBY,
Lake George, N. Y.

## MOHICAN HOUSE,
### Lake George, N. Y.

The Mohican House is situated at Bolton, on the west shore of Lake George, 10 miles from its head, with which it is connected by a pleasant drive along shore and three steamers daily.

It has accommodations for 90 guests, is one of the oldest hotel sites on the lake, near the fishing grounds of the narrows, is a favorite resort for artists and people of culture, and the proprietor aims to make it first class in every respect.

Prices, $15 per week, $3 per day for transient guests. After September 10 the prices will be $2 per day or $10 per week.

A good livery near by.   Address,
H. H. WILSON,
Bolton, N. Y.

## BOLTON HOUSE,

### LAKE GEORGE, N. Y.

BOLTON is on the west shore of Lake George, 10 miles from its head. It is one of the most romantic and attractive places to be found in the country. It possesses rare attractions for the artist in its grand mountain and lake views; for the hunter of partridge and other small game, and the fisherman, in its brook and lake fishery.

The Bolton House, on the shore of the bay, is a new, first-class hotel three stories high; rooms large, well ventilated and well furnished, and will accommodate 60 guests. A roomy observatory on the roof commands an extended view of the Lake to the south and east; the Narrows with its many islands, North-west Bay toward the north, and the mountains on every side.

The large, airy dining-room and pleasant open parlor, occupying the entire main floor of the building, the broad verandah fronting the lake and south sides, boats, guides and fishermen; three steamers, express and mails daily; city cooks and accommodating servants are some of the attractive features of the Bolton House for 1874, as the proprietors have determined to make it the house of the season by supplying its guests with the needs of the present time and age rather than relying on a traditional reputation and the musty events of the past. In doing this no pains will be spared to make the stay of its patrons pleasant and agreeable. Terms $12 to $17 per week. Address,

NORTON & PHILLIPS,
Bolton, N. Y.

FOURTEEN MILE ISLAND.

LAKE GEORGE has long been noted as one of the loveliest sheets of water in the country if not indeed in the world; it is thirty-four miles long, about four across at its widest; surrounded on all sides, excepting at the outlet, by mountains, and said to contain 365 islands. Fourteen Mile Island, one of the loveliest, is 12 miles from the head of the Lake at the entrance to the Narrows; comprising an area of twelve acres of land and mossy rock, covered with a grove of oak, chestnut and Norway pine and commanding an uninterrupted view of the Lake to its extreme head on the south, to Bolton on the west and the Narrows with its hundred islands toward the north. The Hotel has comfortable accommodation for forty guests, and the reputation of setting one of the very best of tables. Three steamers touch at the dock daily, bringing mail, etc. Guides, boats, and fishermen provided if desired. Terms from $10 to $14 per week. Address

R. G. BRADLY & CO.,
14 Mile Island, Lake George, N. Y.

## CHESTER HOTEL,

### M. H. Downs, Proprietor.

CHESTER HOTEL is situated at the thriving little village of Chestertown, 5 miles from the Adirondack Railroad at Riverside, on the direct stage route between Lake George and Schroon Lake; 18 miles from the former and 5 from the latter. It has been noted for years as the center of a great fishing region, and combines all the advantages of a first class hotel, with facilities for rare sport in the streams and lakes near by.

Will accommodate 140 guests. Terms, per day, $2; week, $10 to $16.   Address    M. H. DOWNS,
Chestertown, N. Y.

#### Distances from Down's Hotel

| | |
|---|---|
| To New York | 237 miles |
| " Saratoga | 55 " |
| " Glen's Falls | 27 " |
| " Riverside | 5 " |
| " Pottersville | 5 " |
| " Warrensburgh | 12 " |
| " Lake Pharaoh | 13 " |
| " Friend's Lake | 2½ " |
| " Schroon River (outlet of Schroon Lake) | 2 " |
| " Loon Lake | 1½ " |

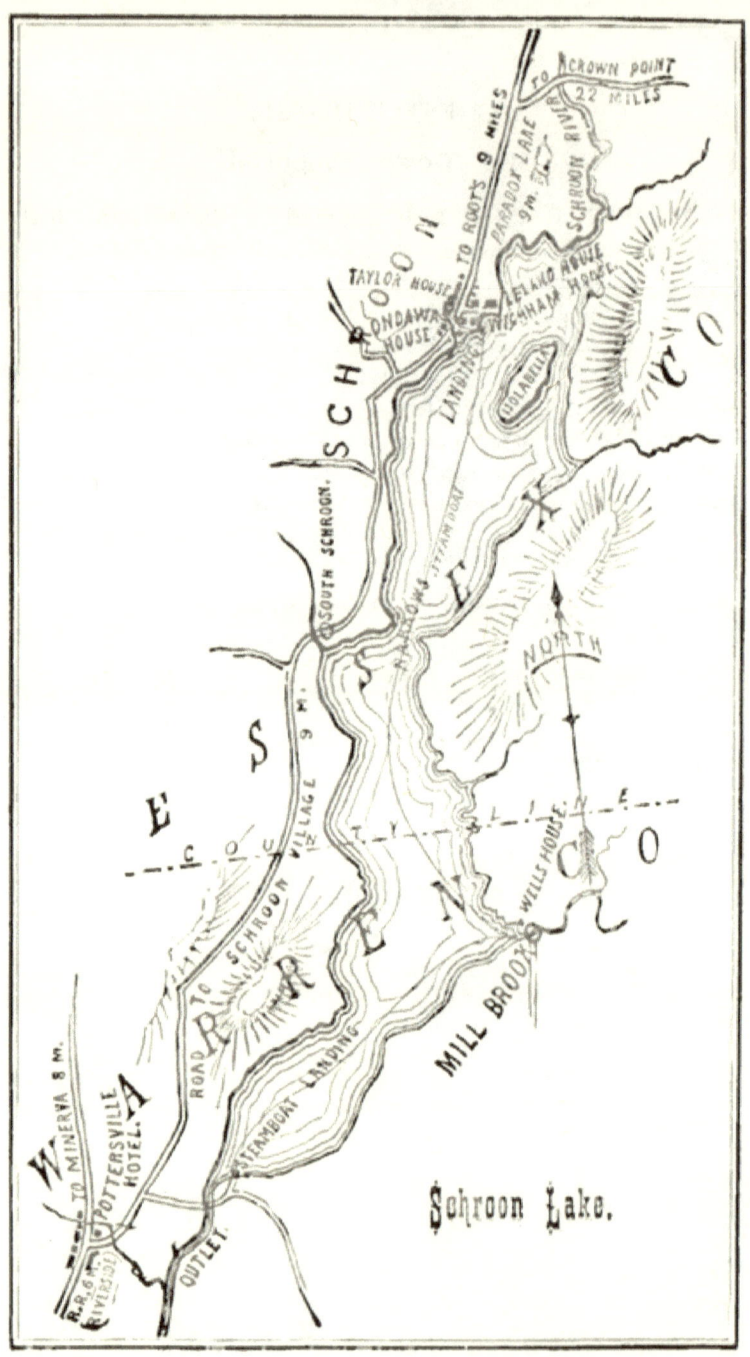

## SCHROON LAKE.

SCHROON LAKE is undoubtedly one of the most popular semi-wilderness resorts in the country. It is surrounded on all sides by mountains — not high, but at the south wild and rugged, broken into curious fragmentary masses, growing smoother as we approach the north end from which the valley of North Hudson stretches away, the mountains on the west growing wild once more, with but one break — at Root's, nine miles from the head of the lake, where the road goes west to the Boreas and Long Lake region — until they come together at Deadwater, and you have to climb up between them to get over into Pleasant Valley on the north. It is nine miles long and perhaps two wide, divided in two nearly equal portions at the Narrows and empties south through the river of the same name into the Hudson near Warrensburgh. At the south end is Pottersville, at the north, Schroon Lake Village.

### ROUTES TO SCHROON LAKE.

New York to Albany by rail or steamer; Albany via Saratoga to Riverside (Adirondack Railroad) by rail; Riverside to foot of Schroon Lake, six miles, in Leavitt & Leland's Concord coaches, connecting with trains; thence nine miles by steamer to Schroon Lake Village. Lake George to Thurman Station (Adirondack Railroad) nine miles by stage; thence to Riverside and as above.

### TIME TABLE.

Leave New York by Hudson R. R. R. at 9 A. M. and 11 P. M.; arrive at Schroon Lake 8 P. M. same day. Leave New York by People's Line Steamers, 6 P. M.; arrive at Schroon Lake 2:30 P. M. next day. Leave Schroon Lake, 6:30 A. M. and 12:00 M.; arrive at New York at 5:30 P. M. same day by railroad, or 6 A. M. next day by boat, and 11 P. M. same day by railroad, or 6 A. M. next day by boat. Baggage checked through both ways.

See route, page 155.

## ROOT'S HOTEL,

### Schroon River, N. Y.

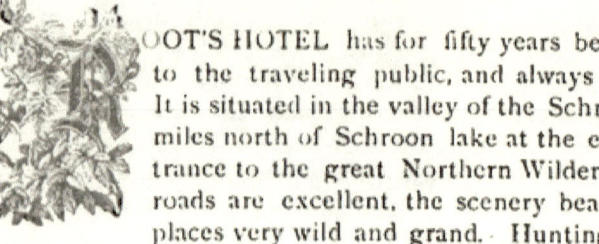

ROOT'S HOTEL has for fifty years been known to the traveling public, and always favorably. It is situated in the valley of the Schroon, nine miles north of Schroon lake at the eastern entrance to the great Northern Wilderness. The roads are excellent, the scenery beautiful — at places very wild and grand. Hunting and fishing is good; and the proprietor intends, as heretofore, to make the table first-class in every respect.

Terms $2.00 per day, $10 per week — will accommodate thirty-five. Address, A. F. ROOT, Schroon River, Essex Co., N. Y.

## POTTERSVILLE HOTEL,

### L. R. Locke, Proprietor,

SITUATE at the south-eastern entrance to the Adirondack Wilderness, near the southern extremity of Schroon Lake. Passengers by stage from Riverside dine here, thence by steamer EFFINGHAM from landing, ¾ mile distant, to Schroon Village at head of Lake.

#### DISTANCES FROM POTTERSVILLE.

To Riverside, (Ad. RR.) 6 miles | To Schroon Village 9 miles.
" Chestertown. 5 " | " Minerva. 8 "
" Lake George. 23 " | " Long Lake. 44 "

Teams furnished to parties desiring to enter the Wilderness from this direction.

Terms $2.00 per day, $10 per week. Address, L. R. LOCKE, Pottersville, Warren Co., N. Y.

## LELAND HOUSE,

### Schroon Lake, N. Y.

THIS is a well-known house, the patronage limited only by its capacity. The table will be bountifully supplied with all the delicacies and luxuries of the season.

W. G. LELAND,  -  -  -  PROPRIETOR.

No bar attached to the house. No pains to render pleasant the sojourn of guests will be spared. First-class accommodation for 125 guests.

TERMS FOR BOARD.—Transient Guests, $3.00 per day. During June and September $12.00 to $14.00 per week; during July and August $15.00 to $17.50 per week.

## WICKHAM HOUSE,
### Schroon Lake, Essex County, N. Y.

THIS new first-class house, comprising a three-story main building, 110x40, and three-story wing 40x22 feet, contains 40 commodious apartments, exclusive of spacious parlors, office and reading room, dining room and halls; is furnished throughout with modern convenience and has ample capacity for the entertainment of 100 guests. It is delightfully located upon an elevation of the lake shore, but a few rods from the steamboat wharf and livery of 50 boats, a short distance from the stores, post, express and telegraph offices and churches, and commands an extensive view of the beautiful lake and picturesque surrounding scenery to the south and east, which may be enjoyed in connection with the promenade formed by the grand piazza, 15 feet wide, 25 feet high, and 100 feet in length upon the south front, from which the grounds slope gently toward the wharf.

Boating, steamboat excursions, pic-nics, and driving, in the most exhilarating climate, and in the midst of the finest hunting, fishing and scenery of the Adirondack region, in connection with modern conveniences, daily mails, and communication by telegraph, steamboat and railway, makes Schroon Lake deservedly the most popular summer resort in northern New York.

Horses, carriages and boats, with drivers, oarsmen and guides if desired, at fair prices by the hour, day, week or season, may be ordered at the office of the house. The steamers *Effingham* and *Libbie S. Benedict* can be chartered at moderate rates.

Schroon Lake is upon the most direct and desirable route to the great Northern Wilderness, and distant but 23 miles ride from the summit of Mount Marcy.

The bill of fare of the Wickham House will embrace all the desirables of the season, with which its tables will be abundantly spread. The proprietor will aim to leave nothing undone for the comfort and convenience of guests.

Board per day, $3; per week, $14 to $21; price depends on time and room.     E. WICKHAM, Proprietor.

## ONDAWA HOUSE,
### Schroon Lake.

THIS old favorite is now in its seventh year, is desirably located in the immediate vicinity of the steamboat wharf, livery of fifty boats, livery stable, post, express and telegraph offices, churches, and principal stores, with first-class accommodations for 90 guests. Comprehensive bill of fare and abundantly spread tables. Guests promptly and respectfully served. Choice wines and liquors constantly on hand. Three hundred feet of piazza fronting the park, lawn, croquet and play ground, afford a delightful promenade, commanding an extensive view of the unrivaled scenery of Schroon Lake.

Board per day, $2.50; per week, $12 to $16. After September 1, $2 per day; $10 per week. Special advantage offered to those who wish to make arrangements for fall hunting.

Thankful for past liberal patronage, the proprietor of the Ondawa House respectfully solicits and will endeavor to merit its continuance. JOHN D. BURWELL, Proprietor.

## TAYLOR HOUSE,
### Schroon Lake.

THIS popular house has been enlarged during the past spring, by a spacious three-story addition of nearly 2,000 feet area, with first-class accommodations for 125 guests. Among its attractions are commodious and well-ventilated sleeping apartments, parlors, office and reading-room, dining-room, halls, barber's saloon, and large hall for amateur entertainments; a delightful central location; new grand piazza; excellent fare; prompt and respectful service; moderate rates. Board per day, $2.50; per week, $10 to $15. C. F. TAYLOR, Agent.

## MUD POND HOUSE.

MUD POND HOUSE is located in the immediate vicinity of the Adirondack Mountains upon the nearest and most direct route, from the south, to the Ausable Ponds and Mount Marcy, distant only about 9 miles, over a good trail, 4 miles of which can be made on horseback. A good carriage road leads to Root's, 9 miles distant. Terms, $1.50 per day. Will accommodate thirty. P. O. address,

M. BRUCE, Schroon River, Essex Co., N. Y.

# E. & H. T. ANTHONY & CO.,
## 591 BROADWAY,

(Opposite Metropolitan Hotel,)     NEW YORK CITY,

Manufacturers, Importers and Dealers in

EVERY THING CONNECTED WITH THE

### PHOTOGRAPHIC ART,

INCLUDING THE MOST EXTENSIVE ASSORTMENT OF

### Stereoscopic Views

**IN AMERICA.**

The Greatest Variety of Stereoscopes,

The Finest Line of Albums,

THE MOST COMPLETE ASSORTMENT OF

### FRAMES AND FRAMING MATERIAL,

THE MOST DESIRABLE COLLECTION OF

### CHROMOS,

ILLUMINATED TEXTS, MOTTOES, ENGRAVINGS,

### Large Plain & Colored Photographs,

Etc., Etc., Etc.

---

Call and examine our unequaled stock of Standard Photographic Productions, and our interesting list of Photographic Novelties.

*For Sale at Wholesale and Retail by*

### E. & H. T. ANTHONY & CO.,

591 BROADWAY, New York City.

# E. & H. T. ANTHONY & CO.,

### LEADING PUBLISHERS OF

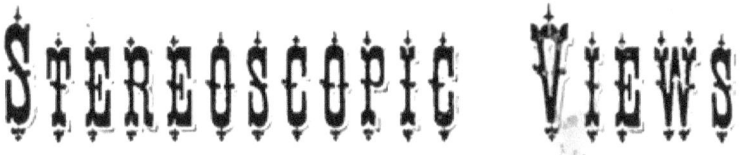

#### IN THE

## UNITED STATES.

---

#### THE TOURIST WILL FIND AT THEIR ESTABLISHMENT,

# No. 591 BROADWAY,

### NEW YORK CITY,

#### THE

## LARGEST COLLECTION

Of these highly popular and interesting pictures, embracing many subjects from the various States of Europe, Asia, Africa and North and South America. Also,

**GEMS OF STATUARY, WORKS OF ART,**

*DIABLES, SPECIMENS OF NATURAL HISTORY,*

#### AND CURIOSITIES GENERALLY,

##### TOGETHER WITH

### EVERY THING CONNECTED WITH THE PHOTOGRAPHIC ART.

# RICHARD WALZL'S
# Photographic Art Palace,

### 46 NORTH CHARLES STREET,

#### BALTIMORE, MD.

---

FINE PHOTOGRAPHY IN ALL ITS BRANCHES, EXECUTED IN STYLE OF SUPERIOR EXCELLENCE.

## Photographic Materials

AND

## *STEREOSCOPIC GOODS,*

#### AT WHOLESALE.

---

Three Medals have been awarded this Establishment for its Superior Productions.

# W. MOULD & SON,

## Druggists,

## BOOKSELLERS AND STATIONERS,

DEALERS IN

### Fancy Goods, Fishing Tackle,

### Ausable Chasm and Adirondack Views,

**CIGARS, CONFECTIONERY, &c., &c.,**

**MOULD'S BLOCK,**

*KEESEVILLE, N. Y.*

| 1874. | Sunday. | Monday. | Tuesday. | Wednesday. | Thursday. | Friday. | Saturday. | 1874. | Sunday. | Monday. | Tuesday. | Wednesday. | Thursday. | Friday. | Saturday. |
|---|---|---|---|---|---|---|---|---|---|---|---|---|---|---|---|
| July. |  |  |  | 1 | 2 | 3 | 4 | October. |  |  |  |  | 1 | 2 | 3 |
|  | 5 | 6 | 7 | 8 | 9 | 10 | 11 |  | 4 | 5 | 6 | 7 | 8 | 9 | 10 |
|  | 12 | 13 | 14 | 15 | 16 | 17 | 18 |  | 11 | 12 | 13 | 14 | 15 | 16 | 17 |
|  | 19 | 20 | 21 | 22 | 23 | 24 | 25 |  | 18 | 19 | 20 | 21 | 22 | 23 | 24 |
|  | 26 | 27 | 28 | 29 | 30 | 31 |  |  | 25 | 26 | 27 | 28 | 29 | 30 | 31 |
| August. |  |  |  |  |  |  | 1 | November. | 1 | 2 | 3 | 4 | 5 | 6 | 7 |
|  | 2 | 3 | 4 | 5 | 6 | 7 | 8 |  | 8 | 9 | 10 | 11 | 12 | 13 | 14 |
|  | 9 | 10 | 11 | 12 | 13 | 14 | 15 |  | 15 | 16 | 17 | 18 | 19 | 20 | 21 |
|  | 16 | 17 | 18 | 19 | 20 | 21 | 22 |  | 22 | 23 | 24 | 25 | 26 | 27 | 28 |
|  | 23 | 24 | 25 | 26 | 27 | 28 | 29 |  | 29 | 30 |  |  |  |  |  |
|  | 30 | 31 |  |  |  |  |  | December. |  |  | 1 | 2 | 3 | 4 | 5 |
| September. |  |  | 1 | 2 | 3 | 4 | 5 |  | 6 | 7 | 8 | 9 | 10 | 11 | 12 |
|  | 6 | 7 | 8 | 9 | 10 | 11 | 12 |  | 13 | 14 | 15 | 16 | 17 | 18 | 19 |
|  | 13 | 14 | 15 | 16 | 17 | 18 | 19 |  | 20 | 21 | 22 | 23 | 24 | 25 | 26 |
|  | 20 | 21 | 22 | 23 | 24 | 25 | 26 |  | 27 | 28 | 29 | 30 | 31 |  |  |
|  | 27 | 28 | 29 | 30 |  |  |  |  |  |  |  |  |  |  |  |

## MODESTY

Is becoming, and may be indulged in with impunity, so long as it harms no one, and does not interfere with business.

Relying on the good taste and honesty of connoisseurs, as well as my own judgment, I can and do say that I have the best photographic views of the Ausable Chasm ever offered for sale, and am willing again to submit them with others to competent judges, who shall decide on their relative merits.

On the following pages will be found leaves from catalogues, which will be sent free, on application with stamp enclosed. I have 600 stereoscopic views of Lake George, Luzerne, Lake Champlain, and other places; also 200 11x14 and 8x10 photographs of the best subjects, many of them designed especially as

### Studies for Artists.

The stereoscopic views are of the large size, mounted on heavy cards, with titles on the front, and will be sold at $2.50 per doz.; small size at $2.00 and $1.20 per doz.; 8x10 photographs $1.00 each; 11x14 photographs $1.50 each. A map of Ausable Chasm accompanies each dozen views of that region. They may be obtained at Fouquet's Hotel, Fort William Henry Hotel, on the steamboats, and of W. G. Baldwin, Keeseville, and at the lower entrance to Ausable Chasm.

S. R. STODDARD, Glens Falls, N. Y., July, 1874.

522. Soldiers' Monument, Glen's Falls.
523. Decoration Ceremonies, Glen's Falls.
524. Opera House — Interior, Glen's Falls.
525. Railroad Depot, Glen's Falls.
526. "All Aboard" — Depot, Glen's Falls.
527. Fountain, Glen's Falls.
528. Fountain, Glen's Falls.
529. Presbyterian Church, Glen's Falls.
530. M. E. Church, Glen's Falls.
531. M. E. Church — Interior, Glen's Falls.
532. Organ, M. E. Church, Glen's Falls.
533. Altar, M. E. Church, Glen's Falls.
534. " Rose " Window, M. E. Church, Glen's Falls.
551. Birmingham Falls, Ausable Chasm.
552. Birmingham Falls, Ausable Chasm.
553. Birmingham Falls from Bridge.
554. Birmingham Falls — Rock in Center.
555. Birmingham Falls — East side.
556. Birmingham Falls — West side.
557. Horseshoe Falls from above, Ausable Chasm.
558. Horseshoe Falls from below, Ausable Chasm.
559. Birmingham Falls from Horseshoe Falls,
560. Birmingham Falls from Horseshoe Falls.
561. The Lodge Entrance, Ausable Chasm.
562. Tower of Babel, Ausable Chasm.
563. Leaning Tower, Ausable Chasm.
564. Split Rock, Ausable Chasm.
565. The Covered Way, Ausable Chasm.
566. Water-worn Rocks, Ausable Chasm.
567. Plume Rocks, Ausable Chasm.
568. The Pyramid, Ausable Chasm.
569. " Boaz," near the Oven, Ausable Chasm.
570. River above the Oven, Ausable Chasm.
571. Looking up from the Oven, Ausable Chasm.
572. The Devil's Oven, distant view, Ausable Ch'sm
573. The Devil's Oven, near view, Ausable Chasm.
574. Looking out of the Oven, Ausable Chasm.
575. Down the River from Oven, Ausable Chasm.
576. Down the River from Oven, Ausable Chasm.
577. Jacob's Ladder, Ausable Chasm.
578. Hell Gate, Ausable Chasm.
579. Under the Wall, near Oven, Ausable Chasm.
580. Devil's Punch Bowl, Ausable Chasm.
581. Mystic Gorge, looking out, Ausable Chasm.
582. Mystic Gorge, looking in, Ausable Chasm.
583. Up from Mystic Gorge, Ausable Chasm.
584. " Moses," Ausable Chasm.
585. Down from Punch Bowl, Ausable Chasm.

586. Down from Mystic Gorge, Ausable Chasm.
587. Stairs to Long Gallery, AusableChasm.
588. The Long Gallery,, Ausable Chasm.
589. The Long Gallery, Ausable Chasm.
590. Point of Rocks, Ausable Chasm.
591. View near Hyde's Cave, Ausable Chasm.
592. Smuggler's Pass, Ausable Chasm.
593. Lower Entrance — looking down into Chasm.
594. Lower Entrance — looking down into Chasm.
595. Stairway, Lower Entrance, Ausable Chasm.
596. Foot of Stairway, Ausable Chasm.
597. Table Rock, Ausable Chasm.
598. Old Bridge at Table Rock, Ausable Chasm.
599. Up River from Lower Stairs, Ausable Chasm.
600. Up River from Table Rock, Ausable Chasm.
601. Up River from Table Rock, Ausable Chasm.
602. "The Sentinel," Ausable Chasm.
603. "The Sentinel," Ausable Chasm.
604. Base of the Sentinel, Ausable Chasm.
605. Sentinel from above, Ausable Chasm.
606. Cathedral Rocks, Ausable Chasm.
607. athedral Rocks, Ausable Chasm.
608. The Anvil, Ausable Cnasm.
609. Easy Chair, Ausable Chasm.
610. Devil's Pulpit, Ausable Chasm.
611. DownRiver from Old Bridge, Ausable Chasm.
612. Gorge from Cathedral Rocks, Ausable Chasm.
613. Gorge from Cathedral Rocks, Ausable Chasm.
614. Gorge from The Sentinel, Ausable Chasm.
615. Shelf Rock, Ausable Chasm.
616. The Walled Banks. The Boat ride — Sunlight.
617. The Walled Banks. The Boat ride — Shadow.
618. The Pool, down the River — Ausable Chasm.
619. "Caught in his own Trap," Ausable Chasm.
620. The Chasm House, Birmingham.
621. Lake Champlain, near Whitehall.
622. Marsh, Lake Champlain.
623. Old Fort Putnam, Lake Champlain.
624. "Put's Rock," Lake Champlain.
625. Lookout Mountain, Lake Champlain.
626. Lookout Mountain, Lake Champlain.
627. Rock Cut, near Whitehall, Lake Champlain.
628. Champlain Canal, near Whitehall.
629. Railroad toward Rutland, Whitehall.
630. Lake Champlain, near the Elbow.
631. "Dancing Water," Bridge at Rouse's Point.
632. Steamer Vermont, Lake Champlain.
633. State-room Hall, Steamer Vermont.

## A WARNING.

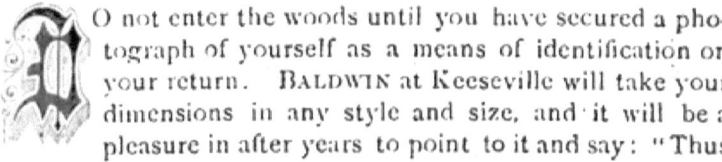

O not enter the woods until you have secured a photograph of yourself as a means of identification on your return. BALDWIN at Keeseville will take your dimensions in any style and size, and it will be a pleasure in after years to point to it and say: "Thus looked I when I entered the Adirondack wilderness, and"—pointing to another which can also be obtained at Baldwin's as he takes both kinds, "*thus* when I came out."

STEREOSCOPIC VIEWS a specialty. A large line of Adirondack and Stoddard's

## "Crystal" Stereoscopic Views of Ausable Chasm.

For sale at the lower entrance and at Keeseville.

W. G. BALDWIN, *Keeseville, N. Y.*

### IMPERIAL ADIRONDACK VIEWS.

(Four by seven inches, $6 per doz.)

1. The Great Peaks from the South.
2. Indian Pass from Lake Henderson.
3. Mount Colden from Lake Henderson.
4. Long Lake, South from Davis Island.
5. The Owl's Head, Long Lake.
6. Buck Mountain, Long Lake.
7. "A Foggy Morning," Long Lake.
8. Mount Seward from Long Lake.
9. Schroon Lake.
10. Boreas River.
11. Whiteface Mountain.

Additions are being constantly made to the list. Large views 8x10 and 11x14 of many of the subjects, designed as studies for artists. Address S. R. Stoddard, Glens Falls, N. Y., or W. G. Baldwin, Keeseville, N. Y.

634. State-room Hall, Steamer Vermont.
635. State-room Hall, Steamer Vermont.
636. Gun Deck, Steamer Vermont.
637. Hurricane Deck, Steamer Vermont.
638. Steamer Adirondack, Lake Champlain.
639. Waiting for the Train, Steamer Adirondack.
640. State-room Hall, Steamer Adirondack.
641. State-room Hall, Steamer Adirondack.
642. Ruins of Fort Ticonderoga, The Barracks.
643. Barracks from the North, Ticonderoga.
644. North Bastion, Ruins of, Ticonderoga.
645. Interior of Officers Quarters, Ticonderoga.
646. Hole in the Wall, Ticonderoga.
647. North from Barrack Window, Ticonderoga.
648. North from Top of Magazine, Ticonderoga.
649. Entrance to Magazine, Ticonderoga.
650. Interior of Magazine, Ticonderoga.
651. Mt. Independence, Fort Ticonderoga.
652. Old Battery on Point, Fort Ticonderaga.
653. Mount Defiance from Fort Ticonderoga.
654. Mount Defiance from Fort Ticonderoga.
655. Tremble Meadow from Fort Ticonderoga.
656. The South Wall, Ruins of Fort Ticonderoga.
657. Site of Covered Way, Fort Ticonderoga.
658. Parade Ground, Fort Ticonderoga.
659. Old Fort Well and Hotel, Ticonderoga.
660. Fort Ticonderoga Hotel.
661. Fort Ticonderoga Hotel from the Ruins.
662. Port Henry, Lake Champlain.
663. Port Henry from Crown Point Ruins.
664. Furnaces From Crown Point Ruins,
665. East Barracks, Crown Point Ruins.
666. South Barracks, Crown Point Ruins.
667. Interior, East Barracks, Crown Point Ruins.
668. Entrance to Parade, Crown Point Ruins.
669. North from Crown Point Ruins.
670. Old French Fort and Chimney Point,
671. Parade, looking West, Crown Point Ruins.
672. "On the Breastworks," Crown Point Ruins.
673. Light House from Crown Point Ruins.
674. Poke-o-moonshine, Adirondacks.
675. View near Poke-o-moonshine, Adirondacks.
676. Whiteface Mountain and House, Adirondacks.
677. North from Whiteface mountain House.
678. In the Wildwoods, Long Lake, Adirondacks.
679. Boreas River, Adirondacks.
680. A glimpse of the Boreas.
681. Mount Marcy, Haystack, etc. from the South

www.ingramcontent.com/pod-product-compliance
Lightning Source LLC
Chambersburg PA
CBHW031826230426
43669CB00009B/1232